A simple trip to the basement jumpstarted for Phil Nero what would become a six-month journey into the history of baseball and perhaps one final attempt at playing the game he fell in love with as a kid.

All he intended was to store a couple of lawn chairs for the winter. In the process he catches a fleeting glimpse of his old baseball glove, just sitting there collecting dust, and growing rigid. He retrieves it, brings it upstairs, and decides to recondition the stiff, shiny lump of dried-out leather.

As the leather softens, he begins wondering not only about the history and evolution of the modern baseball glove, but the unusual connection and oftentimes personal bond between player and this outwardly lifeless piece of sporting equipment.

His curiosity grew.

First he hits the library and the internet. Then, as the glove softens and his knowledge deepens, he considers hitting the road. Why not, he thought, go south for the winter and maybe, for one more season, play a little ball? In this case ball means Super Senior Softball.

With leaves falling, trees growing bare, and another long winter looming, he decides to do just that. But as journeys go, this one becomes so much more than anything he expected or imagined it might. ***For Love of the Glove*** takes readers along for the ride. And what a ride it turns out to be!

FOR LOVE OF THE GLOVE
Why Baseball's the Best

www.philipnero.com

Cover & interior design by Maureen M. Kane of MMK Design, LLC

Library of Congress Cataloging-in-Publication Data
ISBN 9798862899184

First Edition: October 2023

10 9 8 7 6 5 4 3 2 1

For Enzo

ACKNOWLEDGMENTS

Thank you to all my family and friends who contributed encouragement and advice to this modest work. Pat Graham and his pal Bob Albano, along with Denny Darmek, Bob David, Pete Koneazny, Joe Spadaro and David McCraw, provided early chapter reads, ongoing support, and suggestions – Sam Daleo, Gene Laczniak, Sheila Clark, Nancy Hrdlicka, Phyllis Doran, and, especially, Mike Kuchta, who took time to read and review the full manuscript. Mark Rucker not only read some sections, but selected items from his amazing archives, and also offered up his own baseball glove in the process; and Maureen Kane for her enthusiasm and imaginative design. And Mike and Mary Andolina for providing a lake-side artist retreat. There were old friends, new ones, and others I met along the way who not only were supportive, but agreed to share their own stories and love for the game – Randy Quayle, Wayne Heidenreich, Martin Kurtz and so many more. I can't list you all, but I thank you all and trust you know who you are. And finally, a nod to MLB researcher Sarah Langs whose passion for the game inspired the subtitle of this book.

"Take me out to the ball game,
Take me out with the crowd.
Buy me some peanuts and Cracker Jack,
I don't care if I never get back,
Let me root, root, root for the home team,
If they don't win, it's a shame.
For it's one, two, three strikes, you're out,
At the old ball game."

Chorus – *Take Me Out To The Ball Game*

By Jack Norworth and Albert Von Tilzer

FOR LOVE OF THE GLOVE
Why Baseball's the Best

By Phil Nero

"Baseball, it is said, is only a game.
True. And the Grand Canyon
is only a hole in Arizona."
~ George Will

FORWARD

There's something about baseball. I know there are parts of the country and the world where football – both European and American style – has taken root, flourished, and become wildly popular. There are even places where people treat American football, especially at the college and high school levels, as if it were religion.

But there's something about baseball, particularly in the U.S., that makes it uniquely special, even magical. Maybe it has something to do with the number of games in a season.

On the professional level, American football, with its 32 teams playing 17 games in a typical season from early September into January, offers 272 regular season games plus a cluster of additional playoff games leading to the Super Bowl in February.

Soccer (football everywhere but in the U.S.) has numerous leagues on every continent where people engage in sport. Seasons generally begin sometime in August and end the following May. Teams typically play between 34 and 38 games over that period, depending on the league.

American Major League Baseball has 30 teams. Each plays a 162-game season from roughly late March through September, offering a total of 2,430 regular season games plus the playoffs and the World Series. However, a sport's popularity is based on so much more than the number of events and seating availability. Otherwise horse racing would be the most popular sport not just in America, but throughout most of the world.

When I was a kid, I'd take my favorite team to bed with me almost every night. Not the actual team of course – broadcasts carried through the magic of my pocket transistor radio, which I'd hide in presumed secrecy under the covers, listening via the single bud earpiece, the dulcet tones of the announcer's voice lulling me to sleep.

Invariably, I would have to ask my father the final score in the morning. He had this little despair-to-joy prank he'd like to play, telling me my team had lost, before reporting they had really won. This worked fine when they actually did win. Regardless, he loved doing it, even though it drove me crazy. I can't recall how old I was when he finally stopped, or why. Maybe it was after I could, more often than not, remain awake until games actually ended, thus defusing his prank.

My lifelong love of baseball, as encounters with love often go, has had its ups and downs, the most recent complication the result of sabermetrics. This unchecked empirical analysis of statistics, designed to measure in-game activities and alter strategies, changed the very nature of the sport. Mathematicians, left to their own devices, would certainly have ruined the game with things like shifts, pitch counts, load management, and other madness (such as almost eliminating the stolen base and hit-and-run play, for example). Thankfully, with the 2023 season, the powers that be attempted to save themselves from their own insanity with an intervention and an accompanying first wave of rule changes.

I don't blame them for almost ruining the game. Like the rest of us, they couldn't help themselves when they took this object of our collective love for granted. While everyone from owners on down to fans in the bleachers might occasionally waver in our love for the game, it likely will always remain our national pastime, more popular in its own way than any other game or sport, foremost in our hearts and in our thirst for diversions. Why?

Because there's something about baseball.

PART I

FALL

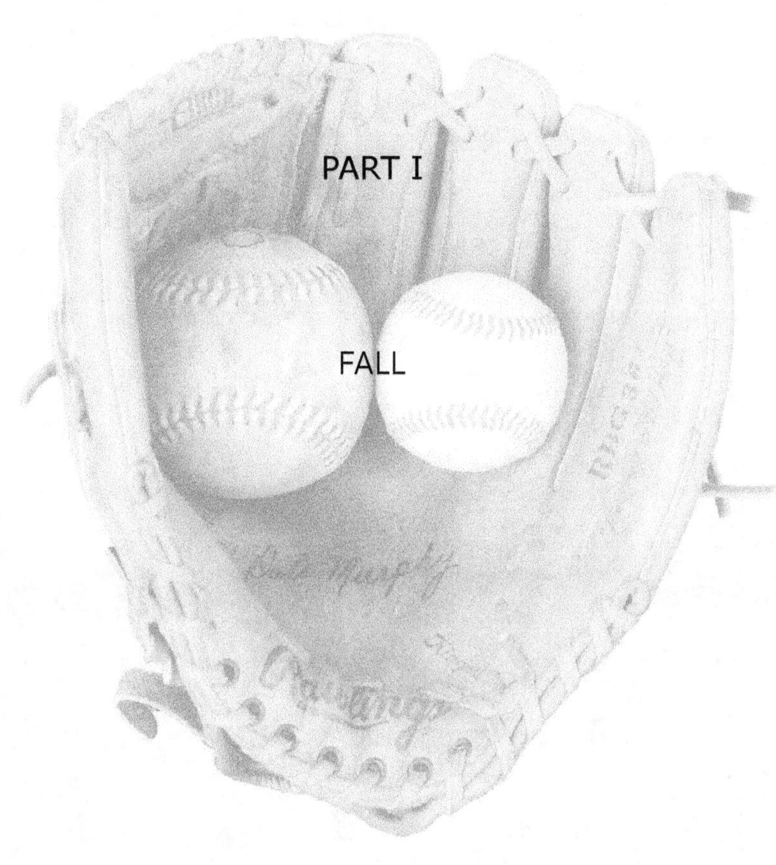

CHAPTER 1

Stand by Your Glove

I wasn't looking for it. It kind of whispers to my eyes and emerges at the edges of my vision. I hardly give it a thought while continuing to haul my lawn chairs to the basement on an otherwise uneventful autumn afternoon. But before turning off the lights and returning upstairs, I retrieve my old baseball glove from its resting place on a dusty, nearby shelf, a simple act that significantly changes the immediate course of what had become my predictable life.

Like its 74-year-old owner, the glove is stiff, dried out some, and showing too many signs of age. I put it on my left hand and pound the pocket. While doing so, a thought begins emerging from those places in our minds where the hitherto unplanned hides. As it takes shape, amid the pounding and the pondering, I reflect on how the many forms and levels of baseball have been with me throughout my life. And I think how they likely will continue to accompany me for what remains of it. I count three years since I last played any form of baseball and begin considering if I might eke one more season not only from my body, but my similarly weathered old glove.

In the process, I also begin debating in my mind whether baseball still deserves recognition as "Our National Pastime." After all, don't the sports pages, talk shows, and other media clearly subscribe to the idea that football gets better ratings and is more popular than baseball? All the print space, airtime, and ongoing coverage devoted to both talk and actual games certainly reflect that point of view. Like it or not, ESPN broadcasts "NFL Today" year-round. The actual player draft in April is preceded by so many mock drafts that it becomes sensory overload for the less-than-overly obsessed.

In fact, ESPN is so organizationally football biased that just before pitchers and catchers report for spring training, it removes the MLB direct link from its website's main navigation bar. Yet despite football's popularity when measured by common metrics, baseball remains – if not the nation's most popular sport, ratings or network-infatuation-wise – No. 1 in how it finds its way into our collective heart, mind, and spirit.

Moreover, it likely will continue to do so in ways that matter most. Sure, football dominates our surface desires for entertainment and engagement. But it's a brutal game characterized by a physicality that panders to an underlying guilty pleasure derived from a level of blood thirst.

Risk to limb and even life to which play exposes the athlete can take a toll on a body that's both subtle and obvious, resulting in physical damage both immediate and incremental. A given player's bone might snap in a moment, ending his career in an instant or, as we'll discuss later, destroy it over time as random joints and body parts slowly deteriorate.

So, despite football's appeal on many levels, its brutality is such that we must sometimes turn away as we watch. Certainly, there are moments of athletic grace, but not without ferocity and pain. Most important, perhaps, is that football lacks baseball's history and isn't nearly as accessible to all. One ensnares; the other enchants.

This enchantment likely begins with the ball which, combined with other elements of baseball's appeal, contributes to an initial attraction football and other sports can't match. Consider too that baseball may possibly be the most gender-inclusive of our popular sports. Tee-ball, for example, is among the first forms of organized play to which parents sign up their boys and girls, and cart them off on Saturdays for socialization and group play. Little League and other forms of our next round of exposure provide youngsters, regardless of gender, an opportunity to engage in fair play together.

When they reach an age that alters the scales of competition, our kids can choose between various forms of softball and hardball activities. Next, for some, the field of play expands from 60- to 90-foot distances between bases – etcetera, etcetera. All things considered, the early universal appeal of baseball's many forms towers over football's touch and flag variations and exceeds the organizational pull of soccer.

So here, in its world of broader attraction, the mustard seeds of baseball's enduring appeal plant themselves alongside life's various rocky paths upon which we all trod, not just in the U.S., but around the world. Even football-crazed ESPN knows this is so. Just look at the lengths to which the network goes in its Little League World Series coverage. Flag, touch, and all other early forms of pigskin play do not enjoy such audience attention, youthful participation, or parental involvement.

As noted earlier, it begins with the ball. Small and spherical, the baseball is a close variation of the very first ball we give our infants. Round and able to be clutched in a single hand, a baseball rolls straight and tends to bounce true. It's the kind of ball with which the smallest of humans can best engage. What cruel parent would first choose to toss their tiny child a miniaturized football? With its weird shape, pointed ends, and inherently irregular bounces, even once cornered and secured, the football is a challenge to grasp, let alone toss back to Mommy or Daddy.

When our little ones get a bit bigger, we might introduce a larger spherical ball into their lives, one that can be kicked, perhaps, as well as tossed, bounced, and caught. Only after all these variations of the round ball do most children engage with something resembling the shape of a football. And by then, some adult in their lives almost certainly has purchased something resembling the tiniest version of our first secondary accessory to any game, the baseball glove.

No parent, aunt, uncle, or grandparent would ever think of gifting a little one some variation of a football helmet and shoulder pads. Nor would they then encourage the banging of heads with another little one. Nor would they ever urge any little human they love to run head down into a swinging door in order to grow accustomed to running over another human sometime in their athletic future. "And hey kiddo, don't drop that ball when your head hits the door!"

In contrast, the miniature version of a baseball glove is likely placed gently on our non-dominant hand sooner than later. Loved ones instruct us how the glove is meant to assist in the art of the catch. The basic fundamentals associated with baseball become part of how we all initially learn to physically engage our world.

So it is that buried somewhere in the deepest, generally irretrievable recesses of the hard drives of our minds, linger memories of intimate, warm engagements with our closest loved ones teaching us to incorporate the tools and skills of baseball into our lives. Consciously or not, from the very beginning, we are linked to baseball's core activities. We're instructed in specific rudimentary practices, then encouraged to expand on what we're taught, all the while learning to play fair and engage positively with each other. That's still a good thing. Isn't it?

This is likely what was at the root of my instinct to hang onto the most recent model of a baseball glove I've owned in my life, along with a baseball and two models of softball, one white and one yellow.

Of course, I have no recollection of my own introduction to spherical objects. Nor do I recall exactly when I purchased this glove, a Dale Murphy model Rawlings RBG 36. Based on Murphy's career, my guess is that it was sometime around 1980 during my medium (modified) pitch softball career in Saratoga Springs, NY. This is a form of softball in which pitchers can throw the ball as fast or slow as they choose with a flat arc of less than three feet or no arc at all. If the arc is too high the pitch is called a ball.

Unlike fast-pitch softball, windmill delivery isn't allowed. The pitcher may swing his arm back and forward in an approximately 180-degree motion or more, but a 360-degree delivery is illegal. This brings up one of the best things about baseball or softball – the wide range and variations to their formats, all of which contribute to making some form of the basic game available for play as we progress through life.

Even stickball, a rudimentary predecessor of baseball dating back to the 1750s, was adaptable in accordance with the environment of its players. Kids using a broom handle and ball created versions of the game playable anywhere from open fields to city streets and schoolyards. Certainly, other sports evolve from past versions and activities as well. But it presents a challenge to come up with one that has done so more than baseball, the history of which involves so many variations of its core basics. Soccer, the original football, perhaps enjoys a similarly lengthy history and global popularity. However, it still struggles to capture a deeply passionate share of the collective American spirit.

How deep is baseball's reach into the hearts of Americans? How creative are they in playing some version of it? How inclusive can it be? How deep is the desire to participate?

I recall watching a New York City stickball game sometime in the early 1960s. A kid with braces on his legs set his crutches against a nearby stoop. He stood in the "batter's box," swung at a pink rubber Spalding ball (often referred to as a Spaldeen) bounced his way, connected and beamed as a fellow player pinch ran for him. Fast forward 75 years and that pinch runner might be playing senior softball someplace and himself be allowed the grace of a pinch runner.

Just as the game connects to players' inner selves, the player connects with baseball's basic equipment. Such is the case with the bat to some degree, but far more profoundly so with the glove. While it can be routine for both kids and adults to share common bats, the glove is so much more personal. With rare exception, in almost every version of the game, players not only possess their own gloves, they're attached to them in a personal way.

In a 1978 single-game playoff to determine the AL East championship, Bucky "Bleepin' " Dent, after breaking his own bat, broke the hearts of Bostonians with a bat belonging to and handed him by Mickey Rivers. Bill Buckner, however, while hobbled by injury, was betrayed by his own glove and human imperfection when he made an error at first base in 1986. The miscue allowed the Mets to go on to win a crucial game and eventually the World Series, again breaking the hearts of millions of Bostonians. Yet he didn't discard his glove.

Unless one's role is designated hitter, we wear our gloves for far more time than we clutch a bat, be it in practice or during a game. Moreover, the time to prepare a bat for hitting pales in comparison to that required for breaking in a new glove. Little League to Big Leagues to weekend softball leagues, this time-honored practice is generally done with love, oil, and a wide range of unusual techniques. Any new, stiff mitt must be coddled, shaped, and made flexible before becoming game ready (though advances in leather conditioning have streamlined the task).

The glove is our constant companion on defense, where we spend far more time than in the batter's box. We intimately slip our non-dominant hand deep into the recesses of its fingers. We rub the outside and pound the pocket with our throwing hand. We even spit on it and rub our saliva into the leather, an act that's totally acceptable by every baseball norm. Nowhere else in our society is spitting so fully expected or condoned, and its benefits endorsed.

In January 2019, a hard line drive struck by an over-60 senior snapped a leather strand holding the webbing of my glove in place rendering it useless. Who would have thought someone upwards of

60 capable of hitting a ball that hard? Rather than borrow another's glove, a piece of shoelace worked to temporarily re-secure the web. After the game, I briefly considered replacing the glove, but instead had it partially restrung. We finished the season together.

Life's demands, followed by Covid and other unexpected events, intervened in any further competitive play related to baseball. I broke the glove out three times at most in the three years prior to fall 2022, usually when my friend Gene, a fellow septuagenarian, expressed a desire to play catch while talking life and baseball. With so few constants in my world, my Dale Murphy RBG 36 endures as a functional connection to more youthful times. Might I even say, more hopeful times?

The letters RBG are also the initials of renowned, late Supreme Court Justice Ruth Bader Ginsburg, a coincidence that provides some amusement, as does the fact that, like my glove, Ginsburg also had a long-running career. Some might say she hung on too long, unlike Murphy whose career was relatively short. He got off to a slow start, but was magnificent throughout the '80s, during which he put up Hall of Fame numbers before suffering a rapid decline and retiring in 1993.

Murphy broke in as catcher in 1976 and played some first base (both unremarkably) before reinventing himself as an all-star outfielder, even winning the National League Most Valuable Player award in two consecutive years, '82 and '83. After nine seasons of greatness, he fell off the proverbial cliff, a decline so rapid it short-circuited what would have been first-ballot Hall of Fame credentials.

His character, however, was unimpeachable. All in all, a fine name to have on a glove along with Justice Ginsburg's initials. I'll also note that I was 36 years old when my first child, Stephanie, was born. Was this glove destined for me or what?

That I pay any attention at all to the name, letters, and numbers associated with those on my glove reflects another factor that contributes to the deeper, enduring affections baseball fans have for the game and its stars over fans of football and its players. Hidden inside helmets and under other protective equipment, football players are less recognizable than their baseball counterparts, and their equipment is far less portable, personal, and endorsable.

College stars don't bring their shoulder pads to the NFL. They don't have their own style or brand of gear. I might see Peyton Manning, Aaron Rodgers, and a few others in ads promoting insurance, shaving aids, and other products. But aspiring young quarterbacks don't wear helmets or other equipment displaying their names the way my Rawlings RBG 36 bears Dale Murphy's engraved signature.

A quick online search of shoulder pads, helmets, and footballs for sale reveals no readily available piece of equipment, new or used, bearing the name of a particular player. A similar search for baseball gloves immediately informs us that any aspiring young pitcher can purchase a Clayton Kershaw Wilson A-2000 glove. And even though Kershaw is a left-hander, it's also available in a right-handed model.

Looking for a used glove, bat, or other collectible? You can get those too, bearing the names of famous and even not-so-famous players. For example, if you want, you can get a glove emblazoned with the name of the not-so-heralded Homer Bush. Although Homer Bush might be one of the best names imaginable for a baseball player, he was hardly a star, at least at the major league level. Still, one can find a marketable piece of equipment that bears his name. At least one such glove still exists; and at least one person retains a connection to the obscure, but speedy, Homer Bush.

Perhaps it's a bit unfair to say Homer Bush was never a star. There are stars we peer at across light years, and there are shooting stars, heavenly flashes in the pan that burn momentarily bright before fading. Homer's brief career in fact offers some insight into several of baseball's enduring and endearing qualities.

CHAPTER 2

Bush, Bo, and a Hippy, Hippy Shake

Homer Giles Bush (born Nov. 12, 1972) played for the New York Yankees, Toronto Blue Jays and Florida Marlins from 1997 to 2002 and briefly in 2004. He was part of the Yankees' 1998 World Series victory over the San Diego Padres. He had the proverbial cup of coffee with the Yanks in 1997 before joining their championship run the following year. In 89 plate appearances over '97 and '98 he batted .378, with seven walks and five stolen bases – speed among his offensive weapons.

In the Series, Bush was utilized primarily as a pinch runner, scoring two runs in the Yankees sweep of the Padres, the team that drafted him a few years before. The Yankees traded him to Toronto that off-season, along with pitchers Graeme Lloyd and David "Boomer" Wells, an exchange that brought controversial pitching ace Roger Clemens to the Yankees.

While on the one hand welcoming Clemens into their fold, many Yankees faithful lamented the loss of fan-favorite Wells, as well as Bush, who on paper showed promise as an emerging star. Still technically a rookie in 1999, he made an immediate impact in Toronto, his first full year in the major leagues. He was so good, in fact, that Keegan Matheson, who covers the Toronto Blue Jays for MLB.com, ranks Bush sixth all-time among rookies in club history, placing him ahead of shortstop Bo Bichette (2019) and first baseman Fred McGriff (1987 and 2023 Hall of Famer), and behind only third-basemen Eric Hinske (2002) and Bret Lawrie (2011). The other five players on the list are pitchers.

A second baseman, Bush batted .320 that year with 5 home runs, 55 RBI, and 32 stolen bases. In the world of analytics, his 2.8 WAR (wins above replacement, FanGraphs) is also noteworthy, coming in the second highest ever among Jays rookies, according to Matheson. The season was Bush's peak as a pro. Hip injuries plagued him. Over the next three seasons, from 2000-02, he played in only 217 games. He didn't play at all in '03 before retiring in '04 after just nine games as a Yankee.

Bush is a poster child for what could have been. In that regard, his career bears contrasting with Bo Jackson's, who is far more widely known and regarded by some as the greatest athlete of all time. Together they illustrate how baseball captures our hearts, and how the physicality of football can either quickly crush, or slowly erode and undermine an athlete's body.

A multiple-sport high school star selected by the Yankees in the second round of the 1982 draft, Jackson instead accepted a football scholarship from Auburn University, having promised his mother he would be the first in the family to attend a major college. At Auburn, he played in star-studded backfields alongside fellow All American running backs Lionel "Little Train" James and Tommie Agee. The latter went on to play on two Super Bowl winning teams with the Dallas Cowboys (and should not be confused with Tommie Agee, a two-time All-Star centerfielder who played with the 1969 Miracle Mets).

Despite his football success, Jackson made it clear his professional pursuits would be in baseball. That didn't stop then Tampa Bay Buccaneers owner Hugh Culverhouse from attempting to woo Jackson. The enticement included providing a private jet flight to a team physical during his senior baseball season. Bucs management allegedly insisted the trip had been approved by both the SEC and NCAA, but Jackson was subsequently declared ineligible for the closing stretch of his college baseball career for the heinous crime of boarding that flight.

An angry Jackson told Culverhouse he would never play for the Bucs and warned him not to waste a draft pick on him. Undeterred, the Buccaneers chose Jackson with the No. 1 pick in the 1986 NFL draft. Jackson rebuffed a $7.6 million five-year contract offer, choosing instead to sign a $1.07 million three-year deal with the Kansas City Royals. After 53 games in the minors at the AA level, he made it to majors in September 1986. In 25 games and 82 at bats, he batted .207 with 7 walks, 2 home runs, 9 RBI, and a .615 OPS.

After two years of steady progress in the big leagues, Jackson began blossoming. He was a starter on the 1990 AL All Star team and won the game's MVP award. He made a stellar catch in left field to save two runs in the top of the first. Leading off the bottom of the inning, he homered in his first All Star Game at bat. In the bottom of the second, he beat the relay on a potential double play, driving in what proved to be the winning run. Then he stole second, joining Willie Mays as the second player in All Star history to have a homer and a steal in the same game. He finished the appearance with two hits in four at bats, two RBI, and a run scored.

By this time, Jackson was a two-sport, star professional athlete. When the Buccaneers forfeited their rights to him before the 1987 draft, Los Angeles Raiders owner Al Davis used the 183rd pick to select him. At first Jackson adhered to his baseball-only stance, but was swayed by a five-year, $7.4 million deal that allowed him to complete the baseball season before reporting to the Raiders, even if that meant missing NFL games. As a result, he played 7, 10, and 11 games respectively in the '87, '88 and '89 seasons. Then, after playing 10 games in 1990 (the same year he was a Baseball All Star Game MVP), Jackson suffered a career-ending football injury in a January 1991 playoff game.

A dislocated hip and related complications resulted in joint replacement surgery. Having been released by the Royals after the injury, Jackson was signed by the Chicago White Sox, but missed the entire 1991 season. He made it back but managed to play only a limited number of games over the next two seasons. A shell of his former athletic self, he retired in 1994 after appearing in 75 games with the California Angels, his third and final big-league team.

What do the relatively obscure Homer Bush and the incomparable Bo Jackson have in common? The answer: football and baseball skills of very high levels measured by just a few degrees of separation. Both were strongly recruited by colleges after stellar high school careers, Jackson by Auburn, Bush by the University of Missouri. Both were powerful high school offensive players, Jackson at running back, Bush at wide receiver, where he posted insanely good offensive numbers.

Bush grew up where the South meets the Midwest at the southern end of Illinois, just across the Mississippi River from the baseball-crazed city of St. Louis, MO. He attended East St. Louis High School, which despite its name isn't at all part of St. Louis, the so-called Gateway to the West. In fact, if East St. Louis had a gateway to anywhere, it was a metaphorical one through which jobs and people left, as they did across the country when America's manufacturing centers crumbled in the 1960s and 1970s. The city became so blighted economically and socially that it and the high school were featured in the 1998 book *Savage Inequities* by Jonathan Kozol.

Bush's football accomplishments were startling, and many of them remain records. As for the quality of the program, Kevin Horrigan, a reporter and later a columnist for the St. Louis Post Dispatch, wrote about the East St. Louis Flyers and their coach, Bob Shannon, in *The Right Kind of Heroes*. The book follows the team's 1990 and 1991 seasons, when it lost and then won back the Illinois state football championship.

Horrigan repeatedly refers to Bush as the team's go-to player. Bush set state records for the most touchdowns and receiving yards in a season and was named to the Illinois High School all-century team.

This returns us to the topic of hip injuries, where Jackson and Bush are metaphorically joined. Hip pointers are among the most common injuries for athletes in many sports, including football, basketball, and soccer, a sport to which an increasing number of American parents are herding their children due to high-contact head injuries associated with football. As troublesome as pointers can be, repeated or harsh blows to the hips can result in bursitis and other chronic, long-term medical issues.

The hip comprises many complex bone structures and is surrounded by a range of muscles both large and small. Pointers result from stress and contact associated with quick stops, changes of direction, falls, and blunt trauma. In football there's the added factor of high-impact collisions and the force of one body regularly landing on another, as was the case when Jackson injured and dislocated his hip in 1991.

No positions in football require more bursts of speed, changes in direction, and body blows than wide receiver or running back. One can only speculate on the root cause of the hip condition that prematurely ended Bush's pro career. However, neither can one ignore the obvious and possible connection. After all, East St. Louis wasn't and isn't any ordinary football program. Its teams play at the highest level and have won national and 10 state championships over the years, while sending close to 20 players to the NFL. Such activities at that level can inflict severe body punishment, resulting in the potential for long-term effects, even (perhaps especially) when younger bodies are involved.

"You can't ignore such connections to long-term chronic injury, or susceptibility to recurrent injuries," says Wayne Heidenreich, MD, a former internal medicine physician and medical vice president with Northwestern Mutual Life. In his role with the insurance giant, Heidenreich was responsible for reviewing individual files and determining whether applicants were good risks.

He confirms that the hip, because of its structural complexity, is particularly vulnerable to sports injuries, especially when running and blunt trauma are involved. This combination is common in rugby and American football, where tackling, piling on, and open-field impacts are combined with bursts of speed and changes of direction. "Even if you remove blunt trauma from the equation, many sports, even those we consider safe, such as soccer, present opportunities for micro-traumas associated with running, kicking, quick changes in direction and sudden bursts of speed."

In soccer, as with football and rugby, there's the added issue of head trauma associated with heading the ball. "Parents should be concerned with this especially with younger athletes whose brains are still developing."

He could not say definitively that the early end to Bush's baseball success was the result of his earlier participation in football. "But it's a logical, even likely, possibility, because over time, these micro-traumas can lay the foundation for chronic hip pain and other issues related to the labrum."

A Magnetic Resonance Arthrogram (MRA) or Magnetic Resonance Imagery (MRI) can help diagnose issues with the labrum, a thin cushion of cartilage between the ball and socket of the hip joint, where most hip injuries (both sudden and cumulative) originate.

"But in most cases, they're not used until after pain presents," says Heidenreich. "In other words, after there is damage, not as a preventive measure."

In the end, despite a truncated career, things worked out financially for Bush. After hitting .320 in his first full season as a starter, he signed a three-year, $7,375,000 contract with the Blue Jays in January 2000.

Bush and Jackson played in an era when football showed very little concern for player health and injuries. The more brutal elements of the game were, to some extent, embraced by fans and teams alike. Players earned nicknames such as "The Assassin." It was politically acceptable for ESPN and other sports outlets to broadcast titled highlight segments with names such as Hits of the Week. Of course, that has since changed. Media attention on player suicide related to head trauma, grotesque injuries to quarterbacks, and paralyzed wide receivers, all helped bring about rules to help protect players.

Although ingrained in the nation's psyche, football's shine and magnetism have diminished somewhat in recent years, even as things like gambling and fantasy teams bolster television ratings and marketability. At the same time, soccer is enjoying increased popularity, especially as an option for parents in search of safer havens for their children to compete. However, from a fan perspective, Americans generally find it lacking in action. Baseball? Well, baseball certainly has problems of its own when it comes to diminished action. A wide range of rule changes for the 2023 season were aimed at cutting down on dead time during the game. These include a pitch clock, regulations to keep batters in the batter's box ready to hit, and restrictions on pickoff attempts. All target pace of play and seek to increase action.

However, nothing contributes to the length of games more than time between innings. Gone are the days when players rush in from the field and pitchers must immediately take their eight warm-up pitches while the leadoff batter exchanges his glove for his batting equipment and quickly gets ready to hit. In times past, when games had more action and sometimes took less than two hours, if the catcher was on base or made the final out of an inning, he rushed to don his equipment while a bench player caught warm up pitches. Today's players leisurely take something approaching 2.5 minutes between half innings before resuming play.

A regulation game requires at least 16 half inning transitions. Coming up with creative ways to continue adding commercial time during lulls in the game and decreasing time between innings would go a long way toward further solving length-of-game issues.

All these and other factors have contributed to an ongoing national debate (or at least a heated discussion) about whether baseball is losing its appeal and is truly our national pastime. And if that's the case, how long can it possibly hang onto that imaginary title? This all makes for a lot of interesting talk.

I enjoy such exchanges and look forward to them, just as I now look forward to a winter reunion with my Dale Murphy Rawlings RBG 36 glove. As I conclude these sentences my glove sits not 10 feet from me, well on the road to rejuvenation, seemingly rejuvenated, and with a voice of its own. "Oil me, oil me!"

It's a voice I can't ignore.

CHAPTER 3

Love and Olive Oil

When I retrieved my old glove from the basement, it still had a ball in the pocket and had retained some of its shape. But the leather had dried out, become stiff, and taken on an unhealthy sheen. Even after removing the ball and laying the glove on its side, stiffness prevented the hinge from fully closing, a byproduct of benign neglect.

As a kid, I learned conditioning a baseball glove begins with Neat's-foot oil. As an adult, the last of my supply had gone the way of many household items in the first stage of downsizing. Surprisingly, however, a quick online search revealed olive oil as a viable option. The first two applications of modest amounts with a small rag supported the claim. Set on its side, the glove began to show signs of coming back to life. Gradually, the leather softened, the hinge began to close.

This act of rubbing oil into leather rekindled an awareness of just how close, even intimate, the connection is between player and glove. There is perhaps no other piece of equipment in any sport with a comparable bond in terms of both dependence and longevity.

Tennis rackets come and go, with some petulant players even smashing theirs in frustration, as if to blame the equipment for weaknesses in their play. In baseball a batter might snap or angrily throw a bat after striking out. But no player would ever rip apart their glove or toss it into the stands after committing even the most egregious of errors. Hockey players routinely use a new stick every game and change their gloves repeatedly within a contest. Football helmets and other game necessities are the purview of the equipment manager. Soccer and basketball require personal footwear and little else. But a baseball player's glove is almost an extension of their personal being.

Ask any sampling of ballplayers at any level about their attachment to their gloves. It's not uncommon to hear some recall even sleeping with their glove as a child. The attachment lingers in so many ways at so many levels. However, no story of bond between glove and player demonstrates the power of the connection more than what Mike Gallego did during the 1989 World Series. Los Angeles Times sportswriter Mike DiGiovanna wrote about it in a June 2011 article.

A utility infielder with the Oakland Athletics, Gallego was so attached to his glove of eight years that he risked his life to retrieve it. The incident occurred when the Loma Prieta earthquake rocked the San Francisco Bay area, interrupting life for millions along with the game and festivities that day at Candlestick Park. Ground shook throughout the Bay area, walls crumbled, roads and overpasses collapsed, utilities failed, and, at the ballpark, things got crazy.

"Power went out. There's complete havoc, and people are yelling, 'Get out! Get out!', Gallego recalled for the article. "We're bumping into things, tripping over chairs, and trying to get out of the stadium. I get halfway out there — I could actually see the parking lot by the door — and I realized, 'Oh, my God, my glove!' So, I turn around and go against traffic back to the clubhouse, to the other side of the room."

Yes, in a move akin to a parent rescuing a child, or an obsessed pet owner saving their cat or dog, Gallego headed back under the stands toward the clubhouse. "It's pitch black. At that moment, I didn't even think; instincts just took over. I grabbed the glove and made my way back outside."

According to the article, the glove was a Rawlings RYX-Robin Yount model, named after the former Milwaukee Brewers star. Measuring 11 inches from the palm to the tip of the index finger, it was perfectly matched to Gallego's defensive needs at shortstop, second, and third bases. Reportedly, Rawlings told Gallego years earlier that he better take care of it because, since Yount no longer played the infield, the company had stopped making that exact model. So, he protected it to the point of packing the glove inside a small plastic shell on road trips to keep it from losing shape inside his equipment bag.

The idea of a baseball glove didn't originate with the beginnings of the game, which contrary to lore, wasn't invented by any one person either. For the sake of convenience and image, some cling to the notion that Abner Doubleday invented baseball in Cooperstown, NY, in 1839. After all, that's where the Baseball Hall of Fame and Museum is located, just down the block from what is now Doubleday Field.

Doubleday hailed from a wealthy upstate New York family, attended West Point, and later established himself as a Civil War hero. The Doubleday myth is one many fans, including former Baseball Commissioner Bud Selig, prefer because – well, it's a very nice myth and a rather pleasant, convenient fantasy. Another single-origin story favors the influence of Alexander Joy Cartwright, himself a serious baseball player who was instrumental in giving the game a key, defining set of rules.

But in truth and logic, baseball's origins predate any single human being. The notion that one of these men, or any human for that matter, single-handedly invented the game is outside the ballpark of common sense. History.com (as do many factual historical references) states that baseball's roots go much farther back than either man, or any other individual – all the way to the 18th century and beyond, when games resembling baseball were first referenced. Regardless of precise dates, there's general consensus that baseball's most direct ancestors appear to be two British games: rounders, a children's game played among early colonists; and cricket, a game the British Empire exported to many of its colonies.

By the time of the American Revolution, various offshoots of these games developed, morphed, morphed further, and were being played in neighborhood schoolyards and college campuses across the country. Increasingly popularized, they became even more prevalent in industrialized cities of the mid-19th century among migrating workers, which is when Cartwright's influence came to bear. He was among a group that founded the New York Knickerbockers baseball club in September 1845. Cartwright, a volunteer firefighter and bank clerk, codified new rules that would form the basis for the modern game.

Among other aspects of baseball as it's played today, Cartwright standardized the diamond-shaped infield, foul lines, and three-strike rule. He is credited with eliminating one of the more dangerous sources of injuries – the practice of making an out by throwing the ball at the runners, striking them directly with a hard, dense spherical object that might as well have been a rock. These and other changes made for a safer, faster-paced, more challenging game that (to the pleasure of many proud Americans) clearly differentiated it from anything of British origin. In 1846, the Knickerbockers played the first official game of baseball against a team of cricket players, beginning a new, uniquely American tradition.

The origin of the Doubleday legend likely grabbed a toehold several decades later in 1907, long after Doubleday's death. A.J. Spalding, a former major league player and founder of the sporting goods manufacturing company still bearing his name, established a commission to determine the origins of the game. Among the stated goals: resolving whether baseball was expressly American (the reality of choice) or derivative of British games (the reality of the obvious). The commission ignored the apparent and relied on information primarily from one man, Abner Graves, a mining engineer who claimed he went to school with Doubleday. By doing so, the commission made myth reality.

Later, the commission's findings came under widening scrutiny, despite occasional support from the likes of Selig. But even the Hall of Fame, which ardently supported the myth for years, has more recently issued statements calling it into question. Today its position offers a bit of a wink and a nod to the entire discussion, while simultaneously praising the commission's findings, and casting doubt on the validity of Grave's account. A four-page paper on why Cooperstown became home to the Hall of Fame includes the following paragraphs.

After the Commission reported its findings in 1907, many of the game's historians disputed Graves' accounts, noting that many of the innovations he attributed to Doubleday were already being practiced earlier in the 1830s. The discovery in 1999 of the original Mills Commission papers, long reported to have been burned, supports the view of many researchers that Baseball developed over time from a long list of other bat-and-ball games. One day, historians may determine that Abner Graves' testimony - covering a period when the widely played game of town ball was undergoing rapid changes - captures that point in time when these changes to the game arrived in one typical American community and caused a minor revolution on the sandlot.

Nonetheless, such a finding will not diminish the Mills Commission's contribution to our National Pastime a century ago. By collecting the memories of many early fans and players while they were still living, the committee created a treasure trove of early baseball history that would otherwise have been lost. Moreover, by identifying a site for Baseball's origin, the Mills Commission initiated the process that ultimately established a home for the sport - the National Baseball Hall of Fame and Museum.

As for the Hall's current position, Rachel Wells, the museum's research librarian, says, "We acknowledge that Abner Doubleday was not in Cooperstown to 'create' baseball in 1839, but rather that baseball evolved over time into the game we know today." She further directs anyone interested in the topic to the history section of the Hall's website.

That some fans remain so passionate about fact and mythology surrounding baseball only establishes further the fervor with which so many Americans approach the game. Moreover, such enduring discussion is also testimony to something inherent to baseball alone. No other sport to which we pay significant attention is so deeply steeped in legend, lore, mythology, history, and tradition. As popular as football has become, as participation in soccer and focus on the game continues to grow – neither can match the spirit with which Americans approach our national pastime.

Measured by such metrics as gambling revenue, TV ratings, etc., we can argue against baseball's status in terms of entertainment and amusement. However, no other sport is close to threatening its position in our collective heart or national history. And no piece of sporting equipment connects physically and emotionally with the players of any game as does the baseball glove.

Born of necessity, the evolution of the baseball glove isn't nearly as controversial as how the game itself developed.

CHAPTER 4

I Haven't got Time for the Pain

As early forms of baseball became more popular, players increasingly realized that catching a baseball with their bare hands, as was the norm, could be abnormally painful. Pitchers may not have been throwing routinely in the upper 90s (mph), but batters hit the ball hard enough to (as the poem "Casey at the Bat" puts it) tear "the cover off the ball."

Historical consensus is that the first gloves players used were likely common railroad brakeman gloves, which they wore on both hands to reduce the sting of impact. The objective wasn't necessarily to catch the ball as it was to knock it to the ground, pounce on it, and make the play. Also, early on, the use of any kind of hand protection generally was seen as a sign of weakness. The country was less than 100 years old. If the British, from whom we had won our independence, didn't need gloves to play cricket, surely rugged Americans, whose strength and fortitude were forging a grand new nation, didn't need gloves while playing baseball. But by the 1870s, as the game grew in popularity, the idea of some kind of hand protection began, well, catching on.

Doug Allison, a catcher with the Cincinnati Redstockings, used a buckskin mitten in 1870 to protect an injured hand. Then there was Charlie Wiatt, a light-hitting, seldom-used, relatively obscure

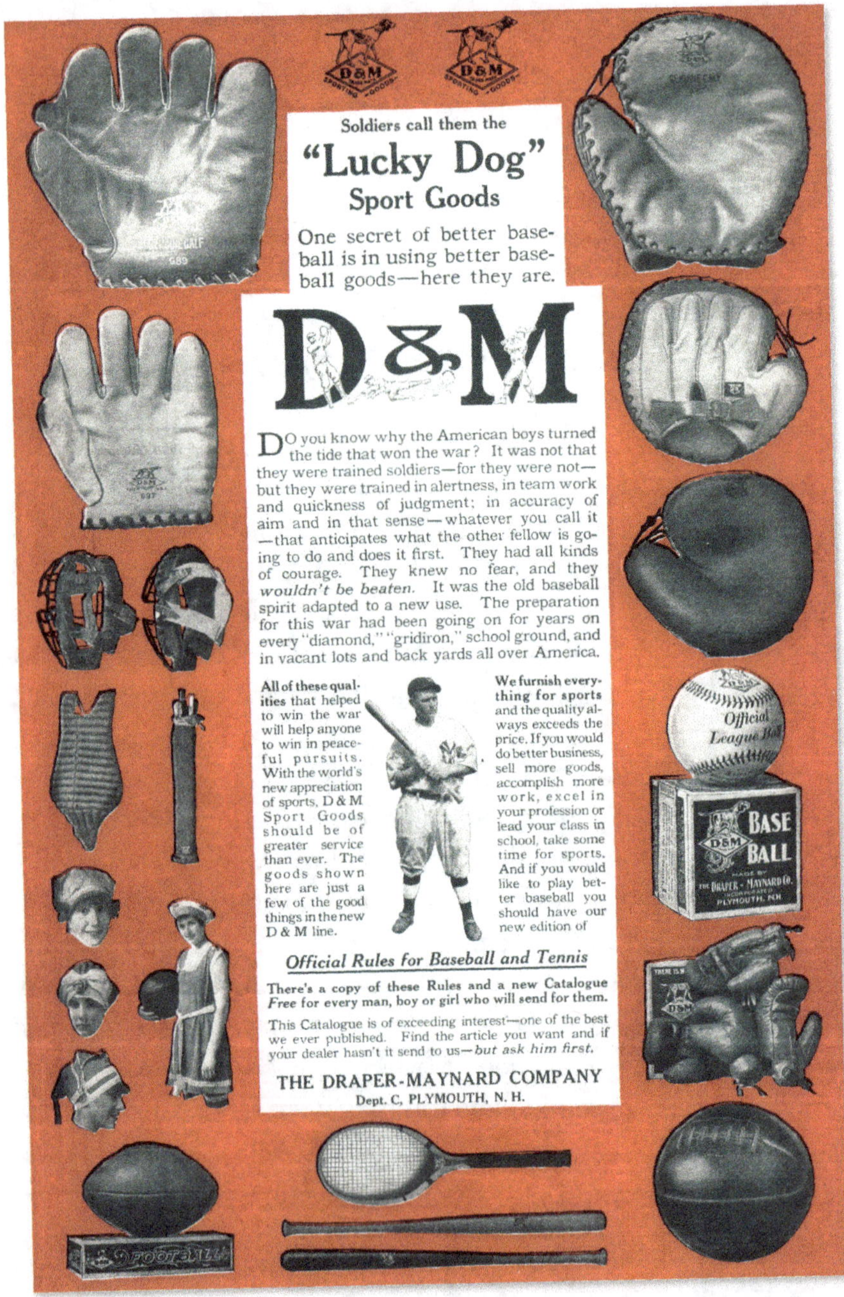

A D&M advertisement from 1919
(Courtesy of the Rucker Archives)

first baseman with the St. Louis Brown Stockings. Little is known about Wiatt, not even if he batted left- or right-handed. He gained attention in 1875 not for his play, but for his use of gloves. Attention, however, wasn't the plan. He specifically used flesh-colored gloves in an attempt to go unnoticed. Other players did notice and derided him. Real men didn't need gloves. Taunts of sissy, and likely more deleterious names, were hurled Wiatt's way.

But yesteryear's sissy is tomorrow's pioneer and, as the game's popularity increased, so did the use of gloves and acceptance of hand protection. This was especially true for catchers, given their unenviable task of catching dozens of pitches a day throughout the season.

Credit for the first catcher's mitt is claimed by two men: Harry Decker and Joe Gunson. While the latter's claim is essentially anecdotal, Decker actually held an 1890 patent for his version, the "Decker Safety Catcher's Mitt." Albert Spalding (he of Mill's Commission and sporting goods company fame, and for whom Gunson once played) was among the first, if not the first, to sell fingerless, padded gloves made specifically for baseball catchers.

One of the earliest pioneers in what would become a global market for other types of baseball gloves was Draper&Maynard, a rural New Hampshire company begun in 1840 to make buckskin gloves, again mainly for work. Things began diversifying when Jason Draper, the son of one of the founders, brought his brother-in-law, John Maynard, into the corporate fold in 1881. From high-quality work, recreational, and dress gloves, the company's "Lucky Dog" brand soon found itself at the forefront of the emerging American sporting goods industry.

It started in 1883 with a request from Arthur Irwin, a shortstop with the Providence Grays. Irwin broke two fingers in his left hand and approached D&M to make a padded, protective glove. He used the glove even after the fingers healed, and continued working with the company to refine it for more effective play. In its heyday – with

A D&M advertisement from 1926
(Courtesy of the Rucker Archives)

the continued evolution, development, and popularity of gloves – D&M boasted endorsements from major league stars including Babe Ruth and Shoeless Joe Jackson, while entertaining several visits from the world-champion Boston Red Sox and other players from around the league who showed interest in D&M product advancements.

This relationship between the company and ballplayers helped D&M not only with product research and development, but also sales and marketing. Player interest assisted in making better gloves and gave birth to the concept of player endorsements. These were initially unpaid, while boosting D&M's growing product line.

For example, in 1910, D&M converted a thank you note from Boston Red Sox leftfielder Duffy Lewis (and his promise that a check would soon be in the mail) into an ad extolling the virtues of their "Lucky Dog" brand of baseball gloves. Lewis played left field next to Tris Speaker in center and Harry Hooper in right, a combination that both Ty Cobb and Babe Ruth called the best outfield they had ever seen. Next to a photo of Lewis, a headline at the top of the ad read: "Wanted, Two 'Lucky Dogs.'" An image of the glove and company contact information anchored the bottom. In between were words and a signature taken directly from the note. "Gentlemen. Received the two gloves that I ordered and I liked them so well that I used one of them in the opening game of the season without even breaking it in."

In 1926, another ad boasted that 42 of 49 players in the World Series between the Yankees and the Cardinals used D&M gloves. Another was bordered with the images of 32 players including Babe Ruth and proclaimed, "This many players can't be wrong." The ad also features images of what appear to be versions of four different kinds of gloves for specialized use at first base, catcher, and two different sizes of gloves for use in the outfield and infield. The company made a practice of listening to players, entertaining and welcoming them to the factory, gathering input, and incorporating what they said into their products.

D&M became a major supplier of sporting goods for professional, college, and recreational use as well for troops during World War I. It made lines of equipment for an array of sports including golf, tennis, hockey, and baseball. Over the years it survived a fire in 1910 that destroyed its factory, growing competition, and the financial pressures of the Great Depression, until closing its doors in 1937.

Meanwhile, leaders in the changing world of baseball gloves included Rawlings. This eventual industry giant joined the forefront of design innovation in 1919 when St. Louis pitcher Bill Doak approached the company with the idea of connecting the thumb and index fingers of the basic glove. The concept and resulting product came to be known as the Bill Doak glove and is credited with transforming the way baseball gloves would be used. No longer simply a piece of protective gear, gloves could now be a tool for enhanced play.

But connective webs on early models were small by today's standards, tiny in fact, and linked only the thumb and index finger.

This glove is representative of those catchers would use in the early 1900s. (Courtesy of the Rucker Archives)

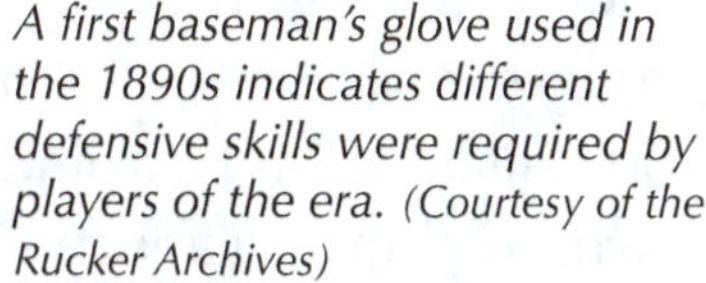

A first baseman's glove used in the 1890s indicates different defensive skills were required by players of the era. (Courtesy of the Rucker Archives)

A fielder's glove from the 1890s – note the size of the webbing and how the fingers were not strung together in any fashion. (Courtesy of the Rucker Archives)

Palms were still large and extensively padded. The remaining three fingers generally were unconnected. In fact, not until decades later, well after the end of World War II, would it become commonplace for all fingers on baseball gloves, be they four- or five-finger models, to be joined at the tips. As late as 1950, an ad for a state-of-the-art Marty Marion glove displayed a model that left the fingers unattached at the tips.

Over time, webs became larger. Glove pockets grew bigger and used less padding, prompting designs that encouraged catching the ball in the web, not the pocket. It changed the way the game was played and elevated attention to player athleticism and defense.

However, when Willie Mays made "the catch" against Vic Wertz in the 1954 World Series; and when the Brooklyn Dodgers finally beat the Yankees in the 1955 World Series; gloves still had not quite made the leap to the unpadded palms, with enhanced pockets, and larger web designs that define today's modern gloves. The major move in that direction came in 1957 when Wilson released the A-2000. Rawlings answered in 1958 with the XPG model. Wilson also dabbled with the Trap-Eze, featuring a long, narrow web that resembled a sixth finger.

Advances made through the last half of the 20th century until now turn balls once destined for the outfield into infield putouts, outfield drives into great catches, and help fielders reach over fences, turning would-be home runs into outs. How big a deal is the evolution of the web? Without it, Ozzie Smith might not be in the Hall of fame, and highlight reels wouldn't include "web gems."

Because of it, hitting .400 and Joe DiMaggio's 56-game hitting streak are likely among the most unmatchable achievements in the game today. Another is Cal Ripken's consecutive games played record, which has nothing to do with the glove at all – due instead to the habit of routinely resting players to prevent injury and maximize efficiency. It even has a term of its own: load management. Of course, most of Nolan Ryan's pitching records are likely also out of reach for the same non-glove related reasons.

With the game having gone through radical changes because of the glove, today's models have size limits. A catcher's mitt can be no more than 38 inches in circumference or 15.5 inches from top to bottom. The first baseman's mitt must be no more than 13 inches long or 8 inches wide. Every player except the catcher and the first baseman are restricted to the use of a glove that is no more than 13 inches long or 7.75 inches wide.

Going forward with these restrictions in place means changes in glove design and performance will be more subtle. Scott Carpenter, a Midwest transplant now living in Cooperstown, and founder of Carpenter Trade LLC, is at the forefront of what he hopes will be the next big thing in baseball glove design: a hybrid glove made of both leather and synthetic materials, and eventually totally synthetic gloves.

He fashions these creations from his "Glove Lab" adjacent to Doubleday Field, just up the block from the Hall of Fame and three stories above the village's Main Street. With a background

Hall of Famer Hank Aaron with a glove typical of those from the mid to late 1950s featuring most of the design elements of today's modern models. (Courtesy of the Rucker Archives)

in fine arts, Carpenter takes up his trade with an artist's passion, dedication, and, perhaps most importantly, creative imagination. His studio is packed with tools, work tables, sewing machines (old and new), computerized equipment, and proprietary innovations he's most careful to protect.

Prototypes and actual gloves collect along the walls in various stages of completion, alongside plaster forms of human hands. To the unaware observer, the space might look slightly chaotic. In fact it's organized in a way that promotes the free flow of imaginative ideas. Carpenter and his assistant, Joyce Whitney, keep regular hours. However, it is not unusual for Carpenter to return to the lab at any time of day or night should a new idea or concept get his creative juices flowing.

Carpenter made the move to upstate NY in 2001 after a brief stint with Rawlings where he studied under glove design guru Bob Clevenhagen. Once in Cooperstown, Carpenter researched the evolution of the baseball glove at the Baseball Hall of Fame and Museum, while spending countless hours mastering the art of glove design and craftsmanship. He determined that the best gloves of the future will be made entirely of synthetic material, not leather. The advantage? They will be lighter, more ergonomic, and easily personalized to the player's hand.

Word of Carpenter's gloves grew and, in time, a few major league players began seeking him out. In 2011, the Hall of Fame Museum acquired a game-used Carpenter glove, citing it as the first all-synthetic glove used in a big-league game and noting it as a new phase in glove evolution. Marucci Sports, a Baton Rouge-based manufacturer of baseball and softball equipment, took note of Carpenter's advancements and acquired his company in 2018. Marucci is a cutting-edge company and an emerging player in a world where Rawlings, Louisville Slugger, Wilson, and Mizuno are traditionally recognized names. The company enjoys a larger presence than most fans, especially older ones, presume.

For example, the sweeping M on the barrels of bats belonging to a growing number of major league ballplayers might be assumed to represent Mizuno. But it is, in fact, the Marucci logo. Company research focuses on the nuances of demand at every level of every sub-category of the game. From the big leagues to Little League and all forms of slow-pitch and fast-pitch softball in between, Marucci's emphasis is on producing superior equipment.

Those most likely to recognize the Marucci M for what it is include players from the college level on up. Easton bats are big among Little Leaguers. But at the major league level, Marucci is king of the hill, or certainly the batter's box.

"Marucci overtook Louisville Slugger years ago in that regard," says Carpenter, who relishes the opportunity to remain in upstate NY, making the best gloves he can. "Now we're making big strides in other equipment too, including gloves. We're making headway. … Their commitment to quality and innovation is what made their offer attractive to me."

For now, that's the Marucci C-2 design, a hybrid leather/synthetic glove into which the company incorporates all the advantages of leather with the most advanced synthetic materials. This results in what Carpenter describes as a "lighter, optimally responsive product," one he believes reflects the perfect blend of the best leather and synthetic fiber materials available.

Sometime in the future, a fully synthetic glove will rule the baseball world, he still believes, but today, a hybrid is the best option. Characteristic qualities he refers to as "memory retention, and the way the ball hits and sticks in the pocket," for example, give leather an edge for now. When a ball comes to rest in the pocket of a baseball glove, Carpenter explains, "it's kind of like the way a person's head is received by a pillow. The fibers stretch and change shape." Afterwards, the leather in a glove returns to its original shape, ready to repeat the task. "It stretches and moves but it will have memory and hold that position you shape it into."

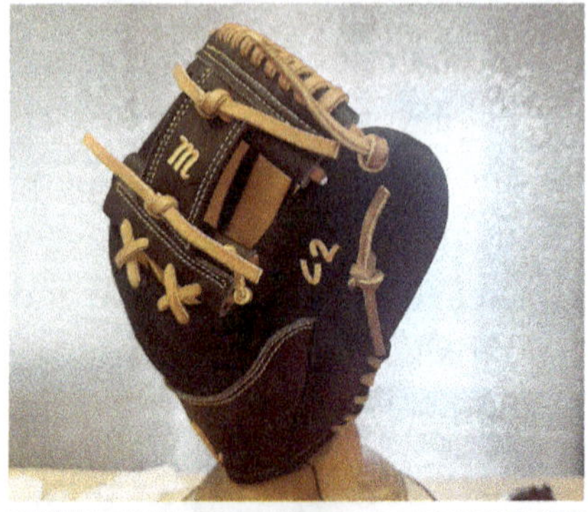

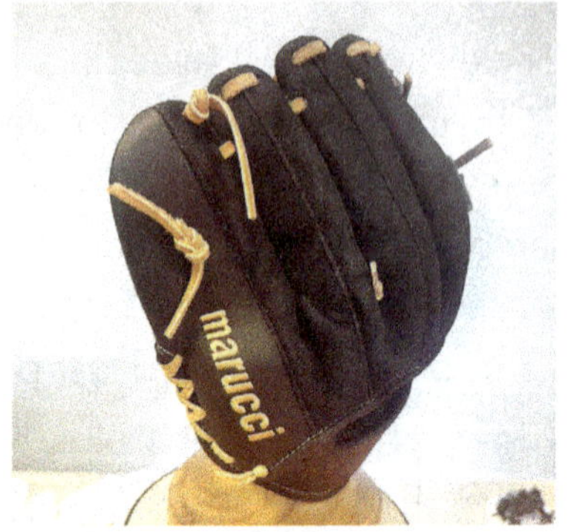

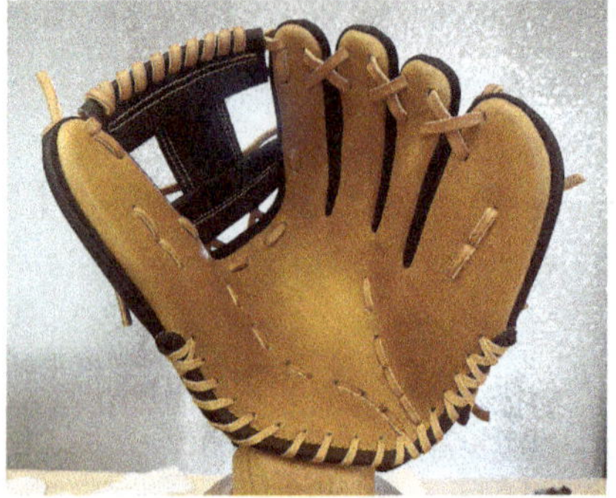

Scott Carpenter uses a combination of natural leather and synthetic materials in the design of his C2 Model hybrid glove for Marucci Sports based in Baton Rouge, Louisiana. The C2 comes in two different models, one for use by infielders and another specifically designed for use in the outfield.

Among his core design principles: the lighter the glove, generally speaking, the bigger the defensive advantage. "When running 40 yards to make a catch in the outfield, having a belt buckle that's eight ounces lighter might not provide a significant advantage," he says, "You don't notice eight ounces there as much as you would at the end of a limb, especially your arm."

It all makes for what Carpenter calls a "faster glove." The glove is "faster" because it's lighter, and the player is able to make quick adjustments and move it more quickly to a different spot. In key moments, such an adjustment might be the difference between success and failure, even life and death. For example, in the case of a bad infield hop, a ball that eludes the fingertips of a heavier glove, might wind up off the fingertips, knocked to the ground or even in the pocket of a lighter and therefore "faster" glove.

In the case of a 110-plus-mph line drive back to the pitcher, getting a glove to a ball a fraction of a second more quickly could

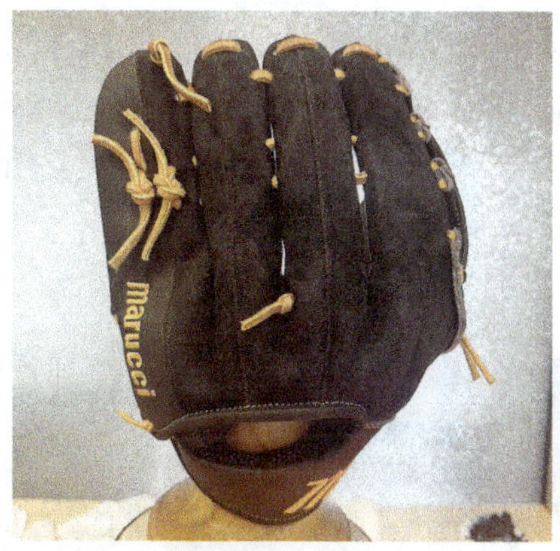

Infielders gloves (previous page) and outfielders gloves.

(Photos courtesy of Scott Carpenter and Marucci Sports)

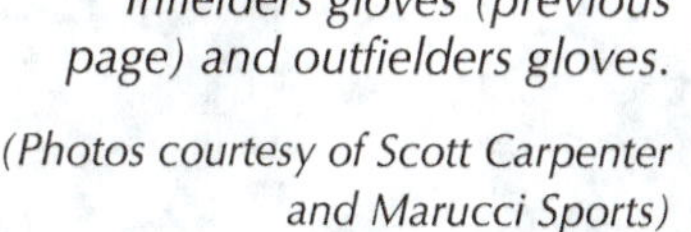

be the difference between deflecting and catching the ball, versus it striking the a player directly, and depending on what part of the body it might hit, preventing a serious, even career-threatening injury.

The C2 also features several unique design characteristics, including the shape and positioning of the thumb in a way that helps deflect and secure the ball into the web and upper palm. Overall, both the infield and outfield models are beautifully crafted pieces of equipment. Despite a hefty price tag reflecting its custom-made qualities and advantages, I momentarily considered purchasing one for my rapidly approaching trip south.

That is until, out of the corner of my eye, I was drawn to where my RBG 36 sat patiently awaiting my attention. It had been over a week since I picked it up, checked on its condition, and nourished it with oil. I wasn't sure it required further attention, but in the moment felt a little guilty. The thought of setting it aside for a different glove felt akin to cheating on someone deserving of my loyalty and devotion.

Scott Carpenter holds the newest version of his C2 outfield glove in his right hand and a used C2 infielder's glove in his left. Studying the used model at his design studio in Cooperstown, NY will provide clues on how to make improvements to upcoming designs. The six-finger oddity is the beginning of a prototype design for use by ambidextrous players.

CHAPTER 5

How Deep is Your Love?

When it comes to one's relationship with their glove, it would be hard to match what my friend Bob has had with his Wilson A-2001. He bought it around the start of his Little League career in northern New Jersey in the late '50s, about the time the A-2000 model made its debut. He used it when he graduated to Babe Ruth League, and while playing on his high school team. He didn't play college ball. But it was by his side and on his left hand whenever he played catch and for as long as he felt inclined to play softball, be it organized or a weekend beer game.

"I'm sure I had some kind of little kid's glove at one point, but it's the only real glove I ever owned," he says, referring to it in the present tense – because he still has it today.

Now living on the West Coast, a ferry ride away from San Francisco, Bob not only still has the glove, but keeps it in plain sight on a bookshelf in his living room with a baseball wedged in the pocket. It's as if he dated other gloves when very young, but upon approaching organized baseball age, his A-2001 became his one true glove. I've known men who married the girl they first met in grade school and dated in high school, but he is the only one-glove man of whom I'm aware. He hasn't played catch or thrown a ball in years. But from time to time, he'll put the glove on, re-introduce it to his left hand, and pound the ball into the pocket in a series of truncated, hard tosses kids instinctively learn to do the very first time they put on a baseball glove.

Bob is among several long-time friends I've kept in touch with over the years and, to this day, we talk baseball at length. Mark Rucker is another. I played ball with Mark in the late '70s and early '80s – softball that is. But as I said earlier, baseball's many forms is what helps embed it in our psyches, hearts, and spirit. And regardless of what form of baseball is being played, the playing skills demanded for each are so similar that players of one know better than to act condescendingly toward players of another.

Any doubters should read up on a four-man, barnstorming troupe of fast-pitch softballers known as the King and His Court. For decades, they took on all comers, allowing the opposition to field a full team against theirs, which included only a pitcher, catcher, first baseman and one fielder. The king (and team pitcher) was Eddie Feigner. He was such a pitching force that he would have been willing to play with just one teammate, a catcher. But that was until he realized at least four players were needed in order to fill the bases on offense and still be able to send up a batter.

On Feb. 18, 1967, the King and His Court played a charity game against numerous major leaguers. The batting order had Willie Mays, Willie McCovey, Roberto Clemente, Maury Wills, and Harmon Killebrew hitting in succession. Feigner struck them all out – in a row. As Hall of Fame Manager Casey Stengel used to say, "You can look it up."

Mark never faced Feigner, but was among the best players on our softball team that put together some respectable seasons of modified (or medium) pitch softball in Upstate New York into the early 1980s. He is also an incredibly talented artist and curator of The Rucker Archive, perhaps the most extensive personal collection of vintage imagery available online for both sale and licensing. It includes high-quality originals and reproductions of hundreds of thousands of images from the 1830s through the 1960s, including several categories related to baseball.

When Mark learned of my plan to head south for the winter to play again, and my efforts to get my RBG 36 back into game-ready shape, he endorsed the idea with enthusiasm. Coincidentally, he was using the same model of glove before giving up playing just a few years ago. Unlike mine, he said, his remained in excellent shape.

Before I could utter the words, "that's a coincidence," he made me an offer he wouldn't let me refuse: his glove. Not 48 hours after entertaining the notion of replacing my glove with a Scott Carpenter hybrid, here came a no-charge offer of a glove just like mine, but in far better condition. Once again, my loyalty was being tested. I decided to accept Mark's glove as a back-up. I'd take it along on my trip south, and if anything happened to mine, out would come its twin.

Mark and I reminisced some about our shared playing days before entering into a discussion about "the soccer vs. baseball thing." Our exchange included talk about the safety issue with football and how a growing number of parents are steering their kids toward soccer out of concern for their health. We talked about gambling and how it will drive people's attention toward one sport or another. We've had elements of this discussion several times before. We agree on many things about how to improve baseball.

Both of us believe the 20-second pitch clock makes sense given some of the time-consuming routines many hitters and pitchers have developed over the years. We think the rule against the shift makes sense too. But we wish hitters would have made it unnecessary by simply slapping the ball to the opposite field, away from the shift rather than stubbornly trying to hit through or over it. That not only would have improved on-base, slugging, and batting average statistics, but also would have boosted in-game action. In the process, teams would have been forced to abandon the shift against all but the most prodigious pull hitters.

When our discussion returns to the bigger question about baseball's long-term popularity, we also come to similar conclusions. We believe TV ratings, gambling interests, and other entertainment and diversionary factors can affect many things, but will fall short of supplanting baseball from its place in our hearts, minds, and national heritage, and thus dethroning it as our national pastime.

This is further established by something I call the Quayle Barometer, as in Randy Quayle, not the best athlete in the world, by any means, but by far the most accomplished all-around athlete I've ever played alongside. Although in his own words "a slow developer," he would grow to be over 6 feet tall, which contributed to his being a four-sport athlete in high school. After making his high school junior varsity and varsity football teams his freshman and sophomore years, Randy suffered an injury, and decided his 140-pound frame was best suited for soccer.

He became an all-county soccer player, while also starring in basketball and baseball, where he excelled at shortstop. I had the good fortune to observe him up-close our senior year when I played next to him at second base. I could occasionally be smooth as suede defensively. But Randy was consistently smooth as fine silk. He was pure fun to watch and play alongside.

I hadn't seen or spoken with him since our 40th high school reunion in the fall 2007, which was also the first time we had talked since graduation. But I called him in 2022 during the FIFA World Cup desperately looking for insight into how I could watch soccer without being bored. People say watching baseball can be boring, and I agree that can be the case these days, given strikeout rates and diminished strategic play. But if baseball (especially prior to 2023 rules changes) is like watching paint dry, it's a fast-drying spray acrylic compared to soccer, which resembles slower-drying oil-based enamel – at least in my experience.

"Yeah, there's not much scoring," he agreed, "It can be pretty boring even for me, but some of the other stuff they do is just amazing." He suggested I ditch my notion that it's a game played mostly with the feet. "You use every part of your body, except your arms. And their coordination is amazing." He compared it to watching professional golfers. "It looks boring and easy on TV. But try to do it yourself and you realize how hard golfing is and how good they are."

One thing about soccer I do find captivating is players warming up, bouncing the ball off their feet, thighs, ankles, chest, and heads, on their own, as well as back and forth between one another. In a way, it compares with the most sophisticated of juggling acts. Randy said he could match that warming up, but better soccer players could elevate it when incorporating the required skill sets into an actual game.

There's a similarity with baseball in that regard. High school, college, minor- and big-league players all look about the same before a game, tossing a ball, stretching, and doing wind sprints. What they do pregame is indistinguishable. The separation occurs when the umpire shouts "Play ball!"

Randy took his soccer skills to Dartmouth. He played at the highest of collegiate levels and post collegiately with a serious amateur team. In fall 1969, less than two years after graduating high school, he took his play, maybe not to a different level, but an entirely different place, Yankee Stadium.

"We dressed in the same locker room Ruth and Mantle used," he said, a trace of dreamy wistfulness in his voice. "It was amazing hearing my spikes clatter on the passageway between the locker room to the first-base dugout, and then walking out onto that field."

Once on the field, he kicked soccer balls on the same grass DiMaggio and other baseball greats roamed. It happened at a time when the New York Football Giants were still playing their games at the stadium, and a few players were also still out on the field. "I shagged punts with Spider Lockhart," he said. Carl "Spider" Lockhart was a popular, all-pro defensive back who played for the Giants from 1965-75. But the lingering thrill of it all isn't that he played soccer there or hung out with a pro football player on his favorite NFL team. No, it was the connection to the spirits of baseball past and ghosts of Yankees greats, some of whom he rooted for as a kid, and others he had heard of but never saw play – legends and idols.

He reminds me this all took place in the late '60s. He was at the original House that Ruth built (where Roger Maris hit his controversial 61st home run) not the 1970s renovated version; not the new sanitized billion-dollar replacement model across the street. This was the original "big ball yard in the south Bronx," as one sportscaster dubbed it.

Or as Randy puts it: "The real Yankee Stadium."

Later, I took his input about soccer and settled in to watch a World Cup semi-final game with a new perspective, attempted patience, and, hopefully, appreciation. I watched with an eye for what Randy called the artistry of the game. I still had no understanding of specific defensive or offensive strategies, but was determined to keep an open mind. I'd spend some time focusing on endurance, full body coordination, and the agility every player must bring to the game, as well as their mastery of the finer points of dribbling, ball control, trapping, and other subtleties. Still, I struggled, finally pressing the DVR record button with a mind toward trying again at some point.

A few days later, I was driving between Minneapolis and Milwaukee during the final game between France and Argentina. I knew the outcome when I turned on my DVR to watch what was being called the most exciting World Cup Finals ever! Ironically, knowing there would be a lot of scoring in the final period, overtime, and a shootout allowed for more interest and less inclination to fast forward than had I been watching in real time unaware of the outcome.

What I found most appealing, however, were the fans and the

air of excitement they created. Unlike a baseball game, people weren't running to and from their seats, getting drinks, grabbing food, and forcing other fans to get up and down obstructing their view and disrupting the experience. There appeared to be no insidious piped-in, high-volume, crowd encouragement noise; no ear-ringing walk-up songs; no eye-popping graphics rimming the mezzanine to make the stadium feel more like the inside of a giant pinball machine or video game than a sporting venue. The game was allowed to be the game.

Good-on soccer for that! And good-on Randy for opening my mind a bit to the so-called beautiful game.

Just as Randy would occasionally awe me with his play as a high school shortstop, I find his post-high-school athletic life pretty remarkable. Minute differences in skill separate the most talented people in so many walks of life. Be it music, sports, acting, or any other field in which some people reach celebrity or high-profile status, what they become and what so many like them become is separated by the finest of lines. There's more to it than talent and ability. There are also elements of luck and good timing. Success goes not just to the most talented or dedicated. A little good fortune and connections can also come into play. In some cases, rules, laws or social constructs are involved.

There are would-be presidents who won popular votes but were relegated to also-ran status by the Electoral College. There are actors who chose one role over another only to see the part they rejected lead to someone else's career-changing Emmy or Oscar. In sports, there's the freak injury. In music it might be the genre a person chooses. Why, for example, is Eric Clapton so highly renowned and financially rewarded as a guitarist, and Sonny Landreath a relative unknown? One could argue the latter has the superior musical chops. Clapton has essentially said as much.

Baseball history is littered with stories of what might have been, especially among Negro League greats who spent their lives in the shadows of fame and fortune because of hate, prejudice, social injustice, and bigotry. Those evils aside, if Pete Reiser hadn't kept running into walls (look him up) or if Roy Campanella had a different last name or taken a different route home in January 1958, how might we speak differently of their greatness or the Dodger's overall World Series record today?

Leo Durocher was Reiser's first big-league manager in his 1941 rookie year with the Dodgers, and also managed Willie Mays when he made it to the majors in 1951 with the New York Giants. Years later, Durocher said Mays was the only player he could compare Reiser to with regard to talent and potential. "Pete had more power than Willie – left-handed and right-handed both. Willie had everything, Pete had everything but luck," he reportedly said.

And so, it's fair to ask, especially in the speculative world of baseball what ifs, with both Reiser and Campanella in the line-up alongside Jackie Robinson and other Brooklyn greats, would the Dodgers have had to wait until 1955 to finally win a World Series

Pete Reiser

Roy Campanella on the cover of Ebony Magazine in 1950, three years after Jackie Robinson broke baseball's color barrier in 1947. Robinson won Rookie of the Year award that year (the first year it was awarded) and Most Valuable Player honors in 1950. Campanella won the MVP in '53 and '55. Note how much more refined the catcher's mitt had become by the mid-20th century.

and beat the Yankees? What would Campanella's final years have been like, and how would the Dodgers have fared in their first years in Los Angeles had he not been paralyzed in that 1958 car crash?

While I may have been blessed or cursed, depending on one's point of view, with a competitive spirit, there's never been the issue of life on the cusp of upper-level athletic success. My life in this regard is lived among the ordinary. Unlike Randy who competed in a chosen sport throughout college and beyond, I took my baseball skills to a small state college and played a single year at the lowest of collegiate levels on a freshman baseball team.

The closest thing to a big-league experience I enjoyed was getting meal money and a bus ride to away games, itself more a minor- than major-league-like occurrence. I had my spikes hung up for me my sophomore year by a coach, who by his own admission, did not select his team based solely on talent. He wanted to keep his better players happy and left some decisions up to one or two, who urged him to select their fraternity brothers to the team.

"It's probably for the best," the coach said in feigned consolation when I challenged the wisdom of his final team selections. "You don't seem like the kind of guy who'd be satisfied sitting on the bench."

"You're right," I replied. "I'm the kind of guy who would have shown you before the year was out that I deserved to be starting."

I guess I had a bit of an attitude, a competitive streak, and no conventional outlet. So along with protesting the war in Vietnam for a few years, I turned to sport parachuting, participating in Mid-Eastern Parachute Association accuracy meets. That meant basically jumping out of a Cessna or other small plane at about 2,200 feet and trying to land on a little red disk about the size of a to-go coffee container lid. Three jumps and the lowest cumulative distance from the target determined the winners. That sufficed until round parachutes were made obsolete by high-performance rectangular canopies that could descend straight down to a feather-light stand-up landing onto a dime, regardless of wind conditions. Accuracy jumping was done as a sport.

So, it was back to softball, along with a developing interest in golf. With golf, to this day, the handicap system and tee box options allow for ongoing competition, but I continue the struggle to improve beyond scoring in the 90s while occasionally — make that rarely — shooting in the mid or upper 80s.

As with golf, flexibility in the rules that allows aging, less supple bodies to continue playing is another contributing factor to baseball's enduring place in our lives and hearts. Relative affordability when compared to golf also helps. Aging bodies can play both, but it's decidedly less expensive to play senior league baseball or softball. It costs about $100 to register for the Collier County Super 60 Softball League. The season lasts about three months, longer if one participates in pre- and post-season pick-up games. There are only a few golf courses within a radius of 50 miles of the league's playing fields that charge around the same $100 or more for just a single 18-hole round.

But my glove doesn't care about my wallet. Its needs are simple: a little attention and a little oil.

CHAPTER 6

To Diminishment and Beyond

I admit to being somewhat dubious when my internet search informed me that olive oil might be a substitute for Neat's-foot oil in restoring my glove to game condition. But I went with what I had, repeatedly working something I associate most with salad dressing deep into the leather and, between treatments, placing a ball in the pocket, securing it with string or a rubber band.

By December, the glove looks and feels great. It's ready. I question if I am.

For the first time in my life, I harbor real concern about injury. Even with all the safety guidelines in place for over-60 softball competition, aging bodies – how does one say it? They're aging. Bursts of speed, leaping, and bending all become more difficult. Additionally, there's the natural order of diminishment. Leaps are less leapy, speed less speedy, and bending – let's just say our toes get farther away from our fingertips and the return upward from a bent-over position gets harder on the knees with every passing year.

I try to imagine where my physical state will place me athletically in the pack of aging bodies that will assemble on opening day, Jan. 4, 2023. I hope for something around the 50th percentile. I recall in 2019 that I was probably between the top 25th to 35th percentiles, but I was also swimming regularly and consistently hitting the elliptical and light weights at the gym. Moreover, I'm migrating south later this year than I did back then. I've also gotten a tad lazier. Make that a six-pack of tad lazier. I've done nothing to maintain muscle tone or endurance other than walk the golf course; and my last round of golf was in mid-November.

Last year I followed the golf season with light workouts in the gym, down from moderate workouts the year before. This year I'm devoid of the personal discipline required to maintain a regular physical exercise regimen. A trainer once told me the hardest part of any workout is "carrying your gym bag to the gym." Whether you're 18 or 80, ain't that the truth!

As I envision the gathering of players on opening day, how I will compare to the pack is replaced by a different thought. I'm suddenly filled with gratitude that I have this opportunity at all. How well I perform, how I compare, whether or not I get injured – none of these things matter. I'm simply overjoyed that I will be playing baseball, or this form of it, which discourages incidental contact while adding three defensive players. In that regard it's similar to town ball, that earlier relative of baseball played all around the states and territories of America in the 1840s, just before Alexander Joy Cartwright codified the rules that led to baseball as it's played today.

Unlike baseball, town ball was played on a square field. There was no foul territory and there were no balls or strikes. Pitchers were referred to as the feeder or giver. Their sole purpose was to lob the ball toward the striker (what we now call the batter) until they swung at a pitch to their liking. Teams consisted of anywhere between 8, usually 9, but in some cases up to 50 or more players. Sides were considered out (when playing the field) or in (when at bat).

Other than the feeder/giver, players in the field had no designated name or area to cover. A ball caught before touching the ground or on one bounce was considered an out. In all other cases, the striker had to run to the corner or base before the ball arrived. An out could be recorded by tagging the base or runner or striking them directly with a thrown ball from any distance and at any speed. A player called out this way was soaked. There was no set number of innings or number of outs allowed per inning.

Thankfully, senior softball, as we play it, doesn't allow soaking and permits up to 12 players in the field: 5 outfielders, 5 infielders, a pitcher, and a catcher. On offense, teams have the option of using a designated hitter, raising the number of potential players to 13.

Batters start with a 1-1 count. Four balls comprise a walk. But once the batter has two strikes, a strikeout can be recorded in three different ways: a called strike, a swinging strike, or after two foul balls. A batter running through first base must run to a mat placed in foul ground adjacent to the base. If there is no play at first, a batter can run to the actual base and round it or continue on to attempt an extra-base hit. These, and other base running rules, help avoid hard contact and potential injury.

For example, if a potential force out is in effect at second or third, runners must veer off to the right of the base to avoid contact with the fielder. If the ball is dropped, or even juggled, the runner is called safe. There's also a second scoring plate, about 20 feet to the side of home to which players must run. Runners are called out if they run to the primary home plate.

The pitcher throws from behind a protective net. Any batted ball that hits the net or the frame supporting it is a dead ball, regardless of how hard it's hit. This can be a very good thing, because while players are generally 60 or older, many of them can still hit the ball very, very hard. The screen has prolonged the health and wellbeing of many a pitcher.

Infielders must be positioned on the infield dirt when the ball is hit. If a batted ball reaches and contacts the outfield grass, it must be fielded by an infielder in order to record an out at first base. If any outfielder touches a ball that is not caught on a fly, the batter is automatically awarded first base and given a hit. However, outfielders can record a force out at bases other than first. And some pinch running is allowed, even for a batter, but the number of times a single player is allowed to pinch run is limited.

These and other minor adjustments make it possible for some players to play well into their 80s, even their 90s in some cases. So long as someone can toss a ball underhand, they can pitch because of the protective screen. As long as they can catch a ball and roll it back to the pitcher, playing catcher is an option.

Baseball is said to be a boys' game played by men. Modified rules allow some of those men (and women in mixed leagues) to remain active while playing a game they've loved since they were children. Even as they age, they can connect with their inner child, and feel, however briefly, like the kid they once were. This is but one among many factors inherent to the game and its history that ensures baseball's special place in our lives.

In considering all the games of sport I've played in my life, none can match baseball. With all its variations of basic play, baseball is unparalleled for the pure joy of it all. It caught hold of me in my childhood; walked with me into my adult years; accompanied me as I walked with my children into their childhoods, just as my father walked with me when he ushered me along to the first crossroads of my life.

Baseball has a history spanning centuries, touching lives past and present. Lives belonging to countless numbers of others and the history not just of a people, but a colony turned fledgling nation, turned model of democracy, turned – turned whatever it is we're becoming today. Baseball is a part of the country itself. Just like country, it is of the people and by the people. That is what romantics of the sport mean when they speak of it being part of the fabric of American life. Not just part of a piece of the fabric, but woven throughout the entire fabric. It's omnipresent in that way.

Documentary filmmaker Ken Burns has taken on a range of subjects in his career. Ask 100 people at random to name a documentary filmmaker, and likely 90 would say Ken Burns. Eight of the remaining 10 wouldn't be able to name anyone. Or maybe 100 out of 100 would say Burns. His film topics include wars (the Civil War, WWII, and Vietnam), famous Americans (Ben Franklin, Lewis and Clark, the Roosevelt family, Jack Johnson, Ernest Hemingway, and Muhammad Ali). And he's taken on baseball.

Some of his films are single episodes. Others are miniseries, comprising as many as 10 episodes, as was the case with Jazz (in 2001) and The Vietnam War (in 2017). In 2019 he covered Country Music in eight episodes. Over the course of his career, Burns' works have bridged nearly the entire history of the United States. He devoted nine episodes to covering baseball in 1994, each representing one of nine innings that make up a regulation game. He followed that up with two more episodes which aired in fall 2010. One was called Top of 10th, the other Bottom of the 10th. Together they cover the years 1992-2009.

Burns was interviewed at a Texas Rangers game in July 2009, at which time he told the interviewer that "the good Lord willing" there would be an 11th and a 12th inning. Including a two-segment film that focused on Jackie Robinson, Burns has already devoted 13 segments to the history of baseball and is hoping to do more. For those keeping score, that's Baseball 13, Boxing 6, all other sports 0. By no means is Burns the barometer for all things sport, but he does want to make films that people will watch. Nor does Burns' filmography represent all that is or isn't popular in America. However, he does have a sense for topics to which people feel a connection that goes beyond what they simply find entertaining.

Baseball may have lost some of its entertainment appeal in recent years, but it remains the nation's most dominant sport when it comes to how deeply it's embedded in our culture, history, and hearts. More Americans attend baseball games every year than any other professional sport because it is far more accessible. There are more games, in more stadiums, with more available seats, under more hospitable weather conditions, over the course of more months of a season, than any other major sport.

I would challenge anyone who cares about such debates to watch only the First Inning episode of Burns' baseball documentary (covering the general history of the game from its roots to modern times) and not be emotionally moved, at least in some small way. In much of his work, regardless of topic, Burns depends on voice-over narration and talking heads. However, the text and personalities he chooses, deliver a quality unlike what we've come to expect from sources such as broadcast and cable news outlets. In Burns' First Inning, narrative quotes draw from Walt Whitman (yes, that Walt Whitman) and Ralph Waldo Emerson (yes, that Ralph Waldo Emerson) to describe the influence of the game on culture and society.

He uses a wide range of politicians, writers, and entertainers, some more familiar than others, but all of whom have something of value to contribute to the topic. I refer anyone who might dismiss baseball's relevance or current status to this First Inning episode titled "Our Game." For the sake of my own modest work, I'll cite a few examples from some of those commentators.

Writer Charley McDowell had this to say: "Baseball has nearly all the qualities and narratives that the country has. It's competitive; it's spirited; it's got joshing and the intellectual side. It's also got labor unions and management, and gimmicks and promotions and venality. [There are] great public fools in baseball, great public heroes, and self-serving people and generous people. And it has pride and unity of towns, and of country." He concludes: "And it'll do as a figure for the American system."

McDowell was a long-time journalist with the Richmond Times-Dispatch and a writer/panelist on PBS television's Washington Week in Review. He passed away in 2010, some 16 years after the Burns baseball documentary first aired. His words still ring true today.

Gerald Lyn Early is a Washington University professor and award-winning author who consulted and appeared in several Burns documentaries, including, Jazz, Unforgivable Blackness: The Rise and Fall of Jack Johnson, The War, and Muhammad Ali; and of course, Baseball.

"I enjoy the game because it's a beautifully designed game. It's a beautiful game to watch. But principally because it makes me feel American; it makes me feel connected to this culture," says Early, a black man. "And I think there are only three things that America will be known for 2,000 years from now when they study this civilization: the Constitution, jazz music, and baseball. They're the three most beautifully designed things this culture has produced."

Whether there would be only three things on such a list or 30 can be debated from now until the artificial intelligence robots come home to rule. But it would be difficult to argue for long, or at all even, if the first three items on a list of any number were the three Early cited.

Then there are the words of John Jordan O'Neil, Jr. born Nov. 13, 1911, in Carrabelle, Florida. He was awarded the Presidential Medal of Freedom posthumously in 2006, the year he died. In between he played for years in the old Negro leagues and came to be known to baseball fans simply as Buck, arguably the greatest player anytime, anywhere, any league. He went on to manage, scout, and work his entire life in baseball, and was inducted into the Baseball Hall of Fame in 2022. Excluded from playing in the major leagues because of his race, O'Neil overcame any bitterness he felt about his exclusion and somehow was able to simply embrace the joy of having lived and breathed every aspect of the game.

"It's an American game. That's just what it is," O'Neil said in his interview with Burns. "I'm 81, but I feel like I'm 15 when I'm talking baseball, I'm watching baseball. This is what it is. It does this to any man. It brings you back."

*Buck O'Neil during his peak years with the
Kansas City Monarchs of the Negro Leagues.
(Courtesy of the Rucker Archives)*

That may very well be the secret of it all when it comes to baseball: it brings you back. Back to the play of one's youth. Back to the time your dad took you to your first big league game and the inescapable awe of staring out across the manicured expanse of a professional baseball field and those immense, towering stands around it. The sounds, the sights, they somehow linger inside to produce an ongoing sense of joy like no other sport.

Be it a game on television, or a glimpse of young people playing as you drive past a softball or baseball field, or rediscovering your glove in the basement and rubbing it with oil and restoring it to life – with its sights, sounds, smells, and recollections – the game brings you back.

A SCRAPBOOK

PLAYERS AND THEIR GLOVES

Roger Bresnahan (19 seasons 1897-1915) and
Jimmy Archer (15 seasons, 1904-18)

John McGraw (16 seasons, 1891-06)

*Arnold "Chick" Gandil (10 seasons, 1910-19,
banned for role in Black Sox Scandal)*

Frank Chance, first base (17 seasons, 1898-1914)

Hank Gowdy (21 seasons, 1910-30)

Jeff Tesreau (1912-18)

Babe Ruth
pitching for
Boston, 1918

Bill Terry (14 seasons, 1923-36)

Babe Ruth
(22 seasons,
1914-35) and
Lynwood
"Schoolboy"
Rowe
(11 seasons,
1932-42)

Martin Dihigo (23 Cuban/ Negro League seasons 1923-45)

Gabby Hartnett (20 seasons, 1922-41)

*Red Ruffing
(22 seasons,
1924-42,
1945-47)*

Dick Bartell (18 seasons, 1927-43, 1946)

Jud Wilson (24 Negro League seasons, 1922-45)

Tony Lazzeri (14 seasons, 1926-39)

*Arky Vaughn (17 seasons,
1932-43, 1947-48)*

Stan Musial
(22 seasons
1941-44,
1946-63)

Early Wynn, 1954 Bowman card,
(23 seasons, 1939, 1941-44, 1946-63)

Robin Roberts
(19 seasons, 1948-66)

Mike Garcia *(14 seasons, 1948-61)*

Mickey Mantle (18 seasons, 1951-68)

A Rawlings display of the modern glove circa 1970 reflecting many features incorporated into present day designs.

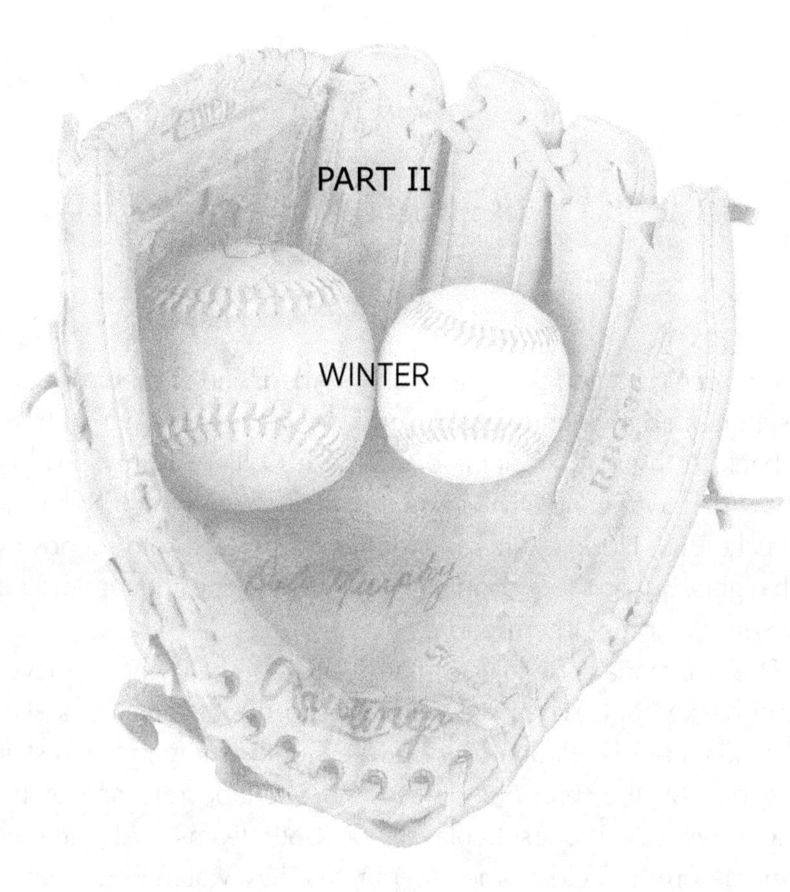

PART II

WINTER

CHAPTER 7

Let's get Real

After three days and two nights on the road, and another evening settling into my winter accommodations, the game would bring me back to the softball fields of northern Collier County, Florida. Getting here was generally a good trip, taking me through Nashville and Lake City, Florida, where I would connect with old friends on both nights. But on the second night, the storytelling and reminiscing met with an abrupt interruption.

The Cincinnati Bengals-Buffalo Bills football game played in the background when we wandered to the kitchen for a slice of homemade pie. Reunion and sweet tooth trumped interest in the game. By the time our bodies and attention returned to the living room television set, players on both teams had gathered en masse on the field, some weeping as they watched a team of emergency medical workers desperately try to revive a player who lay unconscious.

Three days later, Buffalo Bills safety Damar Hamlin remained in critical condition after suffering cardiac arrest in the first quarter following what appeared to be a rather routine hit and tackle. That he was alive at all seemed somewhat miraculous given the amount of time it appeared to take medical workers to restart his heart.

I chuckle when hyperbolic baseball announcers describe

some random player as a "true warrior." Nothing that occurs on a baseball field, or even the more violent environment of a football field, involves being an actual warrior, which requires an avowed willingness to take the life of another human. Nor does being a warrior automatically make one a hero. Marketing and branding have cheapened these things in our modern world. But that's a discussion for another time.

Football players at best (or worst) fall just short of being gladiators. As such, they serve the collective American thirst to be amused and entertained. Football pushes the limits of acceptable violent entertainment. We watch intently, usually without guilt, until something like the Hamlin injury reminds us that our amusement comes with player risk of not just a broken limb or paralysis, but occasionally life.

In contrast, if football players are something short of gladiators in the Roman sense, baseball players are a blend of ballet dancer, acrobat, and gymnast. Now that the beanball is outlawed and hard sliding is regulated, baseball injuries generally all fall into the category of unfortunate or freakish occurrence. A pitch that gets away or a line drive back at the pitcher certainly can put players at occasional elevated risk. But anything life-threatening in baseball no longer, or at least rarely, includes intent to purposefully harm another player for the sake of victory in the game.

In fact, it could be argued that the senior softball players are more gladiator-like than any professional level player. We are a diminished lot, with far more fire in our bellies than fuel in our musculature or flexibility in our limbs. The slightest burst of athletic energy can take a rather large toll. At our age, heart attacks cannot be ruled out.

As I pull into the parking lot on opening day, a radio news report informs me Damar Hamlin remains critically ill in a Cincinnati hospital, on a ventilator, and in a drug-induced coma. The report abruptly concludes when I turn off the car and get ready for the game. After putting on my cleats, I grab my game bag, and, as I walk toward the fields, think briefly of Bo Jackson, Homer Bush, and, for whatever reason, Kirk Gibson. How fortunate they all were to have divided passions between America's game of pastime and our most popular game of amusement and gambling. To varying degrees, they all made more fortunate choices and met more fortunate fates than, say, Darryl Stingley, Mike Utely, Dennis Byrd, and Corey Stringer.

Then quickly the pull of the elysian-like green before me, contrasted against the red infield and warning track dirt, pulls me to what I hope will be the joyful task at hand. I look forward to playing this form of baseball, with all the emerging bliss of a Little Leaguer on the first warm day of spring. I take note to go slow, don't push it, be cautious. I remind myself that while I might be fairly fit for a man of my physique and age (who is no fan of the gym), I am diminished by years and reclining chair. I must stretch, jog, loosen my leg muscles and warm up my arm. Do not overlook or forget these things, I tell myself, or it will be a very short season for me, as well as for my glove, which I remove from my bag and set down in our dugout.

I've arrived almost 30 minutes before scheduled batting practice and decide it would be most prudent to test my legs. So I head out for a jog around the field, a single lap along the warning track. I begin at home and by the time I reach dead center field, my thighs are moaning, and my lungs burn. What has happened to me? A question that is so rhetorical it is undeserving of a question mark.

I push on until I reach the gate adjacent to the leftfield foul pole and casually jog through it before veering left and walking along the grass belt outside the field. I tell myself that this should have been the plan all along – a full lap on the first day makes no sense. I win the argument with my conscience and feel quite pleased with my internal forensics skills. Batting practice is about to present the opportunity to offer my first swings at live pitching in almost three years.

"How do you think that's going to go?" laughs a teammate.

"I'm not too worried. It's not like Nolan Ryan is throwing," I answer. "How bad can I look?" It goes OK, with some solid contact and no swings and misses to make me look silly. Next, I grab my glove and position myself wide of third base to inventory my defensive skills. After several ground balls, I'm satisfied. When I snare a hard grounder moving to my left, I'm further encouraged.

"It'll be nice to have another player out here who can do that," says a teammate. I turn to see the source of the compliment. It comes from Tommy Turton, a fine shortstop and someone I remember being among the top players in the league. When the rosters were first posted online, I was pleased (to put it mildly) that we would be on the same team. In his early 70s, he is lean, fast, flexible, and still hits the ball and the gym really, really hard. I would venture a guess at his exit-velocity, but I so thoroughly detest that and many other sabermetric terms that I'll boldly predict this will be the first and last time you will see it appear in this text. Unless, of course, in a reflection of my age I forget that pledge and use it again.

I'm no Luddite (perhaps a little) but feel terms of advanced analytics belong in the front offices and scouting departments of today's game. Terminology should be used to evaluate players, not be part of the descriptions, accounts and other efforts to describe what happens on the field. Should a curve ball or slider have a lot of movement, I don't need to constantly hear some color commentator tell me the precise amount of vertical drop or horizontal movement in either inches or centimeters. Degrees of launch angle? Please shut up. Use your eyes; see the play; describe the action. I want baseball to be an escape from daily life, not a mandatory advanced math class.

Put such information in a player profile or evaluation file. Publish them or list them where they can be readily accessed if one desires. Use them occasionally, if you must in, any given broadcast.

Just show some restraint. I reject the notion that these might be the words of some old guy admonishing the kids to "get off my lawn." This is a matter of encouraging announcers and commentators to capture the color of the game and the artistry of the players. Their goal should be to add color to what's happening on the field, not wash the green from the grass with wave after wave of analytical bleach.

When we look at the Mona Lisa, do we demand a chemical analysis of the paint and the bonding power of various oils to the canvas?

But I digress. And must resist the temptation to go on doing so!

* * * *

The green and clay-red fields on which we play our senior league games extend like sections of wheels around a central hub of washrooms, water fountains, and equipment rooms, all part of a larger pavilion area. This is where players gather for a brief opening ceremony that includes welcoming announcements, sponsor acknowledgments, a brief invocation, and an abundance of doughnuts, coffee, and Gatorade.

I recognize and say hello to several players from my team of three years ago. Without any provocation, each of them shares the sentiment I expressed earlier: the 2019 Orioles of the Collier County Super Senior Softball League was the best team any of us had ever played on in our lives. Not the most successful – simply the best in terms of team chemistry and competitive joy. They reassure me that my reasons for returning to play another year are more than valid.

But it's time to replace the orange shirts of Orioles past with the maroon and grey of Phillies present. I rummage through the ones yet unclaimed for a large. I reject the first because of the number: 13. As a Yankees fan, it makes me think of Alex Rodriguez. No need to say more. After a small and two extra-large, I come across another large. I turned it over to reveal the number 7. As a Yankees fan, it's a keeper. Again, no need to say more.

Following a few additional warm-up tosses and another round of stretching, it's time to take the field. I've been slotted into the 6th spot in the batting order and assigned third base. I grab my glove from a familiar resting place above the green bat rack affixed to the fence adjacent to a gate that opens to the field. As the home team, we're assigned the third-base dugout. My position is a few short strides from the bench. I slide my glove onto my left hand. The fit feels perfect. The leather, unlike on that fall day when I retrieved it from my basement, now soft, moist, and flexible – the pocket deep and wide. Practice grounders thrown by the first baseman slide easily into the mitt. Glove and player (given our respective conditions, suppleness, and flexibility) are as ready as we'll ever be.

I inhale deeply, breathing in the moment. The morning sun is warm; the sky a bright blue; the grass still slightly damp with what remains of a morning dew; the red infield dirt on the moist side and dustless. All forces internal, external, and historical align, as Buck O'Neil put it so well, to bring me back. I have no doubt that every player on the field is experiencing their own version of being brought back. Perhaps not as fresh as mine, but it strikes me that every game, played or observed, involves some level and form of being brought back. The day becomes not about winning or losing, but the process of being there.

From my position at third base, I watch each pitch, observe the batter, anticipate contact and direction, and move with the play. Then I get ready and repeat, repeat, and repeat again. Four innings pass before a ball is hit my way. Still, there are things to do: direct relay throws, call out the number of outs to other players, cover my base for possible plays, back up throws from the outfield, chase foul pop ups, at least for a few steps until it's clear they're unreachable.

On offense, there is plenty of action for both teams. In my first four at-bats I walk once, get two hits or "credited hits" (those that require some level of misplay short of obvious error) and one pop out to third base.

Runs are plentiful. A pattern develops. They score, we take a slight lead. They score; we tie or take a slight lead. Both teams are limited once by the five-run rule, under which scoring is capped at five runs or what is required to tie a lead greater than five runs in any given half inning. The limit remains in place until the ninth inning when the restriction is lifted, and a rally of any size becomes an all-you-can eat scoring buffet.

The same general ebb and flow of runs continues until the bottom of the fifth. We score two runs to take a one run lead and have the bases loaded with two outs. Next comes what appears to be a bases-clearing hit toward the gap in left-center. Our man on first takes off and has enough speed to catch up with the runner on second. As they approach home, he must even slow down not to pass him. That gives us five runs for the inning and what appears to be a significant four-run lead.

But there's a lot of screaming from the opposing players gathering near first base. They jump up and down pointing at the base, insisting the runner left before the ball was in play. Our on-deck batter walks toward the dugout shaking his head in total agreement. "It wasn't even close," he says. "I don't know what he was thinking." The runner guiltily agrees, whispering, "I don't know what I was thinking either."

The umpire doesn't need to hear the quiet admission and declares the runner out, by rule on a force play at second. None of the runs count. Instead of a large lead, we hold the slimmest of advantages. Back on the field, we kick the ball around and throw it to the wrong base enough for them to score twice in the top of the sixth. With two on and one out, I position myself well wide of third base, daring the batter (who has been dinking us to death going to right field) to pull the ball.

He takes up the dare and hits it hard on the ground just to my left. I take two steps, reach and watch the ball head past me toward left field. I look up expecting the worst, only to see the best possible of outcomes. Tommy, who had made one of the earlier errors, hadn't moved at all when I shifted from my normal spot. Reverting to his usual stellar form, he snared the ball smoothly, ran toward second waving off other fielders, stepped on the bag, and fired the ball to first, completing a clean, inning-ending double play. We leave the field trailing by just one run in a game that's producing them in abundant clusters.

As can be the case with any form of this game, be it stickball, softball, whiffleball, baseball/hardball* – take your pick – the pattern of play suddenly changes. We go in order in the bottom of the sixth. They do the same in the top of the seventh. We fail again to score in our half inning. They put two men on in the top of the eighth, but also fail to score. A game that had produced 37 total runs and a 19-18 score through six and a half innings of play yields no scoring for two full innings.

But ignore the age of the players. Ignore that we're playing softball and the play is somewhat south of consistently stellar. Ignore the outcome, because it also doesn't really matter beyond the confines of this small patch of earth. The only thing that matters is that this is our game, our form of our pastime, and this band of 25-plus, 60-plus-year-olds is joyfully playing it. We're caught up in it. It has brought us back to caring and playing. And though it only matters in this infinitesimally small scheme of things on this tiniest little diamond-shaped swatch of dirt and grass – in this tiny moment, in this tiny place, it has brought us back.It brought us back and, in the end, we came back with two runs in the bottom of the eighth and a shut-down 1-2-3 top of the ninth on defense

*Note: Throughout this book the term "hardball" will be used at times to distinguish baseball from other variations of the game.

for an opening day 20-19 win over the Orioles. And, at least for a little while, the outcome matters to the 2023 Phillies of the Collier County Super 60 Softball League.

Later I linger in the parking lot making small talk with Tommy and a few other hangers on. I'm about to close the trunk and leave, but first I place a ball in the pocket of my glove. "We did good," I think to myself. And before the trunk is fully closed, I repeat the same words softly to my leathery extension of body and spirit. "We did good."

CHAPTER 8

Aches on Aches and a Side of Sore

I'm sore Thursday morning, the day after the game. Every muscle from my buttocks to my toes has aches in their aches. On the other hand, from the waist up, arms and shoulders are doing surprisingly well. I hope that, with four days until we next play, even this old body will have enough recovery time. By Saturday things begin looking up for me, but more importantly, also for Damar Hamlin, the Bills' defensive back, who is now conscious, breathing without assistance from a ventilator, and communicating remotely with his teammates back in Buffalo.

In five days he went from near death, freakish injury, and cardiac arrest to well on the mend. Sports coverage that had been discussing the horrors of physical football play, what that says about our society, and what on God's Earth we should do about it returned to the more routine talk about playoff chances, point spreads, and outcomes of a non-medical nature.

Soon after, Hamlin is transferred to a hospital in Buffalo to continue his recovery. Details about the young man's well-being are vague. He's talking, but still considered in critical condition as doctors speak hopefully about his improvement, while remaining wary about the ongoing condition of his major organs. There are several soap-opera-like articles about the so-called tension between

NFL office executives in the immediate aftermath of the injury and whether play should have resumed. There's finger-pointing and accusations about who and what created on-air confusion over the possible resumption of play. But two things are clear. Not only could Damar Hamlin have died, but future games will go on without skipping a beat or a week.

Had the greater tragedy struck, flags in stadiums might have been flown at half-staff. There likely would have been on-field ceremonies, flyovers, moments of prayer and silence. Players would have worn Hamlin's number 3 on their helmets and sleeves. We can only guess what else might have been done. But we know the games would have gone on, because, as a nation, we are consumed by football, and team owners demand their revenue streams. The NFL show continues at all costs. The Super Bowl is king of all spectator events and price per 30 seconds of advertising time. Long live the many sports books and office/barroom pools that compete for the gambling dollars. From the $2 bettor to the high rollers and betting addicts, football consumes us.

In contrast, we choose to immerse ourselves in baseball's softer, gentler, kinder appeal. This isn't to say that baseball ownership doesn't have its share of blowhards and dollar worshipers, or that its history isn't marred with its own share of flawed moments and actors. From Comiskey to Yawkey to Schott – on and on it goes. Still, baseball is more of a choice we make. It's a wider, slow-moving river in which we decide to swim, float, and take pause for the long, downstream journey, not a raging current in which we're caught and swept away. Sure there's gambling on games, their outcomes, and moments of internal action. But the atmosphere feels different.

In football, fans stand up and scream for a score. In baseball, fans, in addition to standing up and screaming for a score, often kick back and keep a scorecard. In football, we keep time. In baseball, we pass time. It is our respite. It is our societal balm. It is our pausing by the woods on a sun-soft day, which is, in retrospect, what I wish I had done on day two of the Collier County Super 60 Softball season.

All seemed fine as I walked onto the field. Even the result of the game, a 24-16 victory over the Dodgers, was all I and my fellow Phillies teammates could have hoped for. But physically it was a disaster for my body and for the bodies of two other teammates as well. Going in, our first baseman, Gary Rocco, was already dealing with an emerging problem with plantar fasciitis. Within three innings of play, three more of us, me included, would come up lame. The result: large gaps and deficiencies in our defense, and pinch running demands galore on offense. They were the kind of injuries you see all the time, primarily muscle pulls, twists, and strains. The thing is that you don't often see so many of them all at one time.

The score implies we stormed to victory. The truth is we limped there, and none so quickly (or should I say limply?) as I. On the very first play, against my better judgment I volunteered to switch positions with an outfielder and promptly pulled my left quad and groin while chasing a ball headed toward the gap. I was back at third base after that and, two innings later, a line drive reminded me of what Scott Carpenter had to say about the potential benefits of a faster glove – you know, that eight ounces at the end of a player's arm can, in certain circumstances, be significant. If a ball is hit hard, a move with a lighter glove could get to it just a fraction of a second more quickly; enough to make a difference.

You might also recall what I said about some of these guys: though they might be old, some can still hit the ball really, really hard. Well this was a bullet! What's the exit velocity of a bullet-like softball? I don't know and don't care. All I know is that my Dale Murphy RBG 36 had made it from my left knee to just inside the instep of my right foot when the ball struck me squarely on the outside meat of my shin, maybe three inches above the ankle.

I also know that it stung. Then it hurt. Then I felt like screaming.

But of course, I didn't. Instead, I channeled my inner badass jock, grabbed the ball, and looked around to see if there was a play to make anywhere. Then I raised my arms to call time. Glove on the left hand, ball in the right, arms high, I walked toward the pitcher on the mound.

"That's gotta hurt. You OK?" he asked.

"For now," I smiled and winked. "But I'll let you know later if it's true when they say, 'that's really gonna hurt later.'"

About 18 hours from then I learned just how true it can be. After waking up at about 4 a.m., I started making my way to the ol' water closet. I felt a twinge of pain in my left groin from the pulled muscle there, but nothing approaching the fiery jolt just above my ankle when I shifted weight to my right foot. A slow and cautious trip to the bathroom followed. After taking some Tylenol, I lay in bed experimenting with stretches and finding a comfortable position. Eventually I fell back to sleep and, by morning, the Tylenol had kicked in.

A bye on our schedule for Wednesday allows me a full week to recover. Additionally, it affords the unexpected opportunity to be an umpire, a who'd 'a thunk it moment for me. The flu and Covid had taken a toll on the league's all-volunteer umpire crew. When the call for help came from the league's (also volunteer) commissioner, saying no didn't feel like an option. I may have strayed from the Church, but that Catholic guilt lingers, and there are no regrets in this case that it had.

Umpiring anything other than tee ball where kids have little knowledge regarding rules and still fully trust the adults in their lives had been the sum of my experience till this point. On the player side of things, I recall often shaking my head in disgust over the ineptitude of the men in blue. I still hold professional umpires to a standard that allows me moments of fan rage. However, let's give the recreational guys a lot of slack. Here are just a few plays that reflect why.

A runner is safe at home by two steps. But remember, to prevent collisions and injury, the scoring plate is about 20 feet from home on the third base side. An ump must do their best to be in a position to see both plates. All plays are considered force plays. The runner is safe by at least a step. But the defense claims he missed the plate and they call for an appeal. I have no idea if he did or didn't miss the plate and let the run stand because it wasn't close. Oh, the abuse!! Fast, furious, but brief, as their manager reminds them that (a) I'm not a regular umpire; and (b) it was early, and the play wasn't close. Good man, I thought to myself.

When the runner in question went out to play the field, he admitted that he had missed the plate. He apologized for not saying anything and went to his position at first base, where a short time later there's a bang-bang play. From my vantage near home, it could have gone either way. I call the runner safe to the outrage of the team in the field. When the half inning is over, the first baseman pauses near home plate en route to the dugout in order to assure me the runner had been out.

"I could've gone either way," I reply. "Make-up call for your play at the plate, and you got the better end of the deal." He laughs and nods in agreement.

So, in my brief, informal career as an umpire, I got to piss off both teams, indulge my fallibility with a make-up call, and acquire a sincere appreciation for volunteer umpires everywhere. That still is not the case for their major league brethren. Among my many complaints about the well-paid, big-league gang in blue, number one is the notion that different umps can have different strike zones. The strike zone should be the strike zone. One ump should not be allowed to say he's got a wider or lower one. Define it. Train everyone to call it uniformly. Anything else is self-indulgent, look-at-me nonsense.

Equally absurd is the idea that a veteran pitcher gets more leeway on strike calls than a rookie. Why should someone with more experience be granted any latitude just because they've been around longer? If anything, it should go the other way, like horse racing does with the five-pound weight allowance for apprentice jockeys. When home plate umps finally lose their pitch calling responsibilities to strike zone robo-umps at the big-league level, I think it will be a better day for baseball, so long as each player is measured, and everyone's particular zone is programmed into the system. And come Monday game time, I hope this hobbled former umpire, with five days to heal, can get his legs right; or at least somewhat functional.

By Saturday, things are looking up for me injury-wise. I can walk without a limp and decide to take a ride downtown for what I believe will be a crafts fair in Cambier Park. In addition to open green space, the site includes an outdoor stage for concerts, tennis courts, and a softball field, where I happen on a clinic for about 20 young players enrolled in the Naples Girls Softball League. It's a no-nonsense affair (but not at the expense of fun). At the center of activities is an incredibly knowledgeable young woman, Meagan Rembielak, a former standout player at Appalachian State University in Boone, NC from 2010-13.

"I come from a baseball family. My Dad was a Division I coach. I've played all my life," she says later. "This is what I do. It's in my blood." Clearly what is in her blood is transfused via passion into her younger charges attending the day's event, all of whom play Naples Girls Softball. With the clinic completed, they linger on the field to talk and grab some photos with their new mentor. Their collective mood is a combination of awe, thirst for knowledge, and likely a little bit of wouldn't it be great if you were my mom or older sister?

For Megan, the clinics started as a way to maintain a connection with the game she grew up loving, and without professional playing options after college, perhaps provide a different career path linked to the sport she loves. Her fiancé, part of the Florida Marlin's front office organization, urged her to film some of her drills and broadcast them on a YouTube TV channel. In time, her efforts evolved into MegRem Softball, a business and method for teaching the skills of the game to young girls.

Of course, what Megan teaches is not slow or medium pitch recreational stuff; it's fast-pitch, highly competitive softball. She travels up and down the East Coast and throughout the South and Midwest giving clinics at a pace that continues to grow. A quick check of her website reveals a schedule of 11 clinics over about a month that includes five stops in Orlando, New Milford, CT, Waterford MI, Elkhart, Iowa, and Hoover, AL.

"I'm doing better than I ever would have dreamed," she says. "I can't imagine doing anything else."

Megan Rembielak demonstrates proper hitting technique at a girls softball clinic in Naples, FL.

I walk away thinking how great what I just witnessed is for the game of baseball and the larger community formed by the variations of ways the game is played. Regardless of gender or the size of the field, I feel myself taking a different view of the game's offshoots. It's all baseball. It's the same game. The size of the field may differ along with the size of the ball and participating players, but it is all baseball. This appears especially true when contrasting baseball (played on a diamond with 90 feet between bases and a 60-foot-6-inch mound-to-plate distance), and a softball field (with 60-foot base paths and a pitching rubber set 43 feet, 3-inches from home). Or in the case of Collier County Super 60 Softball play, 70 feet between bases.

On average, and by most accounts, pitchers at the Women's College World Series throw underhand, windmill style pitches that rise and dip at an average speed of about 63 mph, but can top the radar gun in excess of 70. Adjusting for distance, release points, arm extension and other factors, a 63-mph pitch is roughly equivalent to 91.1 mph from a typical high school, college or pro baseball mound.

Baseball pitchers rely on a combination of speed, control, and movement. A pitcher cannot live by fastball alone, with the exception of Mariano Riviera, who got away with it because he mastered a cut fastball that darted with late movement, both in and away from the batter, and usually with pinpoint control. Similarly, pitch spin allows softball pitchers to create movement in pitches that rise and dip in different directions. The fastest softball pitch ever recorded by a woman was 77 mph by Monica Abbott in 2012. However, some of her peers and others who relied on a combination of less speed, but more spin and movement, have recorded superior pitching statistics.

This train of thought gains further steam as I recall the game I had umpired a few days before. One of the teams included two women, one of whom stood out as among the best all-around players on the field. Yes, Collier County Super 60 Softball is a co-ed league, but fewer than 1 in 20 players are female. They play by all the same rules with the exception of age eligibility, which is 50, as opposed to 60 for their male counterparts.

Though slightly smaller than most of the men on the field, Ann Koenig is among the most fit and fastest of all. In the batter's box, she's all confidence and business, but tends to smile more than most of the men and seems to play with a greater sense of joy and appreciation for the moment. She may lack the power of some guys, but possesses a solid, athletic swing and hits the ball harder than many. She kicks at the dirt, digs a firm toehold, and aggressively attacks the pitch. On defense, a backhand play in short left field to snare a sinking line drive that had appeared to be an almost certain hit keeps the game within reach for her team, though they would ultimately lose.

Five days later, when we take the field as opposing players, her solid play, both in the field and as leadoff hitter are key to handing us our first loss. Even without the benefit of advanced statistics, there's an argument that she could be her team's best player. On our team, male-egos-be-damned, I'd be happy to make a wager and take up the argument that she would be our third best. I think an argument for second wouldn't be a stretch either. But now is not the time. It's a three-month season and we need to build team chemistry and confidence. Emasculation in any form or subtlety wouldn't help. Our team and season, both of which started out so promisingly, has hit what one might call a speed bump. Or should I say what we hope is a speed bump, as opposed to a Florida sinkhole.

We followed the loss to Ann's team with another two days later, in which we showed an alarming inability to catch the ball in the field and hit with any consistency. What felt like an offensive juggernaut our first two games had gone wherever juggernauts go to hide. We are injury-prone and in an early season tailspin. Watching brings to mind the words of Casey Stengel when he managed the hapless

New York Mets in their inaugural 1962 season. "Can anybody here play this game?"

I think we can. I know Ann Koenig can.

She grew up on a large farm in the tiny town of Whiting, Iowa. "I've been playing ball since I was four or five," she says. It began on an open swath of the family farm. When chores were done and the weather allowed, she and her siblings would don their caps, grab a bat, ball, and what gloves they had and play a game called 500.

It's a game that reached peak popularity in the late 1950s and '60s, when kids rode their bikes or walked around their neighborhoods, going door-to-door, scrounging up enough bodies to go to the park and play. The rules are simple. One person tosses a ball in the air and hits it toward the cluster of fielders who scramble to catch the ball on the fly for 50 points, or after it hits the ground for 25. The first fielder to accumulate 500 points gets to bat until someone else accumulates the requisite total. Sometimes, if there are enough players, the last person to bat assumes the role of batting practice pitcher, before getting a chance to play and compete again for another turn at the plate.

Now 59, Ann stands 5-feet-1-inches tall and weighs a fit, muscular 135 pounds, 5 pounds more than in her prime playing days. Back on the farm, there were enough brothers and sisters growing up together to play 500 anytime there was time. "I was the little kid keeping up with my brothers."

She describes the western Iowa of her youth as "a girl-sport-friendly state" in which she could play mini-league softball beginning at 7, followed by maxi, and then organized school teams. Her first aha-athletic moment came in the sixth grade. She made a great play on a line drive and received her teammate's praise for the effort. Growing up with a domineering and often difficult father on a farm where hard work was not just expected but demanded, the concept of accolades was a foreign one.

"I liked it," she says, as if confessing a sin of indulgence. Affirmations launched her on a fast-track to success. She fell in love with softball and had opportunities to play both fall and summer schedules. "From eighth grade on I played varsity. We might not have had the best coaches (in rural Iowa), but we had a lot of support." With that support came an approach to the game that has guided her since. "I learned to play my best but accept all else." At times that included jealousy. "I beat out a senior for shortstop when I was a sophomore. Some of the girls hated me."

Playing ball and a rough home life have something in common: both require making constant adjustments. So, she pulled her hat down low on her head, something she does to this day, hid behind the brim, made herself smaller than her already diminutive frame, and focused on her dream of playing Division 1 softball.

Enjoying team and individual success at both the regional and state levels, that dream seemed well within reach. But in her senior season, she injured her back and needed surgery. That meant no scholarship and a summer lost to recovery. Dreams slipping away, she started dating the son of a farmer one county over from her family farm. Both farms were the largest hog operations in their respective counties.

A life of hog farming, however, was not on her wish list. She wanted to play Division 1 softball, not repeat her mother's life. She "ran like hell," taking refuge with her Aunt Jeanette in Ames, not far from the Iowa State campus, where she registered for classes, focused on her rehab, and started thinking of a future that would likely involve trying to play as a walk-on somewhere.

That's when her stars suddenly realigned in fortuitous formation. Her older sister, Donita, called from Amarillo with news that West Texas State University, in the midst of transitioning to Division I football, was caught in a Title 9 crunch. Faced with a need to invest in women's sports, the school was desperate for softball players. "They had to quickly form a team," says Ann. "I got a decent scholarship."

Always a stellar defensive player, Ann tailored her offensive game to her most effective skills – speed and contact. "I was basically a bunter. I got to swing away maybe once every three games." But bunting in women's fast-pitch softball in the early 1980s wasn't what you might think. In a game where runs were at a premium, teams relied on players who could take a range of approaches to putting the ball in play, running fast, getting on base, and placing pressure on the defense. She mastered a small arsenal of techniques that included not only conventional bunting, but several half and three-quarter swings at a variety of angles designed to, as the saying goes, hit it where they ain't.

"I knew I wouldn't be a star," she says. "I just wanted to play up." Still, on one of those rare occasions when she got to swing away, she took advantage of the opportunity to fulfill one of her college goals – earning a coveted $100 home run bounty. Unbeknownst to the NCAA powers that be, a team supporter had a standing offer to the West Texas State women's fast-pitch softball team: hit a home run and earn a crisp, clean, C-note. Ann's chance came in her sophomore year against Texas Tech. Given a rare opportunity to swing away, she connected with a towering drive that rode the wind, high into the sun, and beyond the reach of the left fielder. Ann sprinted off on contact.

"I'm rounding second and the ball is still coming down," she recalls with a wide, 20-tooth grin. From there, she turned on the jets, rounded third and headed hard toward home. The throw beat her by two steps. The catcher went low to apply the tag. Ann went vertical, leapt over the catcher, avoiding the tag and scoring a $100, inside-the-park homer.

The college game has gone through a lot of changes since then and, with the exception of her height and weight, so has Anne. "When I played, a lot of games were one to nothing. It's still not a high-scoring game, but things have changed. There's more power. Runs are less scarce."

Ann Koenig shows excellent form as she takes batting practice prior to a Naples Super 60 Softball game.

When her college career ended, she hooked up with a competitive, slow-pitch league for several years. In one of those seasons, her women's team came out of a tournament losers' bracket, went on a streak, and won a double elimination, Class B State Championship. She enjoyed competitive co-ed opportunities as well but, by the early 1990s, family responsibilities intervened. There was no time for any form of the game.

"I took up jogging," she cracks.

Twenty-eight years later, following a move from Austin to the less densely developed reaches of northeast Naples FL, Anne stumbled across a small, slow pitch co-ed pickup league. She unearthed her old glove (the same one she used in college and the early '90s) and resumed playing. That was September 2021. By January 2022 she joined the Super 60 (but women can play at 50) Collier County Softball League.

"When I'm out there, I don't feel like a girl, I feel like an athlete," she says.

When she resumed playing, that inner athlete immediately kicked in. Not content with just playing again, she decided to work on her game. In her words: "I really prepped in." That meant working out, watching videos, and dedicating herself to improvement. She changed everything about her hitting approach. "Every two weeks I'd add a new thing." In September of 2022, "It all just sort of coalesced."

And now, she's "just playing the game again." She's playing it, however, as well or better than most of her peers, male or female. She plays four days a week: Tuesdays and Thursdays with a more competitive league; Mondays and Wednesdays with the likes of us. She's not concerned with how many years it might last, she's simply happy to be playing.

"I'm just here and now," she says. "One good play, one good hit, I live on that for a week. I feel like I'm 25 years old."

Or as Buck O'Neill put it: "It brings you back."

CHAPTER 9

All Roads Lead to Baseball

Following a weekend in which the sports world is focused on Week Two of the NFL playoffs, the fourth week of Collier County Super 60 Softball League play begins with a rainout. I get the news on my way to the fields. There are clouds here and there as I ponder what to do with my suddenly wide-open Monday morning. Before I make the decision to head to my favorite coffee shop, more clouds gather and the heavens open wide.

But soon I'm settled into a small table sipping a cup of hot coffee and enjoying a cinnamon scone. I hook up to the Wi-Fi and begin skimming through the day's headlines on my smartphone while eavesdropping on a nearby conversation between two fans discussing the previous day's Buffalo Bills-Cincinnati Bengals playoff game. They were talking more about a single spectator than the game.

"He looked like a ghost behind all those snowflakes, making love hearts with his hands," said one.

"Well, they played like something was haunting them," said the second, in reference to the Bills, who were flat, disappointing, and seemingly incapable of making in-game adjustments.

The "he" under discussion was Damar Hamlin, the Bills player who suffered cardiac arrest when injured in the game between the same two teams three weeks earlier. They, of course, were his Buffalo teammates who lost the game along with their chance to advance in the playoffs.

"Maybe they know more than we do. You hear he's doing better, but he's on oxygen. Then you hear nothing. The sports shows talk about him a little, but does anyone know how he's really doing?"

"I kinda think maybe the NFL doesn't want to discuss it until after the Super Bowl. You know, even if he's OK, it's still not great for their image."

Their conversation reminds me of my encounter with a young mother during Megan Rembielak's clinic 10 days earlier. The mom had one eye on her daughter on the field; the other on her 2-year-old son having a ball sitting and playing in the dirt next to it. The kid was as energetic as he was adorable, tossing plumes of loose dirt into the air like a mini Lebron James launching talcum powder before a basketball game.

"You must have a daughter out there," I say.

"Yes. The one in black." She turns and points to the field. The girl in question shifts her feet, moves laterally back and forth, getting herself in position to make imaginary fielding plays. We talk about the boy and whether he shows any interest in sports at this point. It turns out he grabs and throws any kind of ball whenever there's an opportunity. We agree that he's destined to follow in his sister's footsteps and will be playing tee ball early on.

"What about football?" I ask. She immediately rolls her eyes and starts talking about the Hamlin injury, and hopes even if he makes a complete recovery, he thinks twice before entertaining a return to pro football. As for her own son, she has no intention of encouraging him to take it up.

"You know, with the head injuries and all," she says. If he develops an interest on his own, however, she's not sure if she'll prevent him from playing. For now, it's a matter of waiting and hoping it doesn't become an issue.

As I leave the coffee house and replay all these events and conversations in my mind, I allow myself a pseudo-psychic moment.

Not a data junkie, more of a tea leaves reader, I have no doubt that football will continue to garner attention as a sport with enormous entertainment value, but participation will decrease. Gambling revenue will soar. Quality of play will be fine, because while participation might drop percentage-wise, there will be a more-than-adequate player pool. Like a car wreck on the highway, traffic will back up from the rubbernecking, but observers will move along down the road, relieved not to be part of the scene or directly connected to it in any way.

Meanwhile, back on the softball field following Monday's rainout, our team seems happy to be playing and in good spirits despite our two-game losing streak. Injuries, combined with an infusion of two players, who've recently arrived in town, provide an opportunity to tinker with our defense. I'm plugged in at middle infield, which had been error prone our previous games. The position requires controlling the area around second base and working both sides of the bag, depending on hitter tendencies. While no one will confuse me with Rogers Hornsby, it's an area of the field with which I'm both familiar and comfortable covering. With our best player Tommy still at shortstop, we enjoy a boost in up-the-middle defense and stop giving away extra outs in an area of the field that gets a lot of action.

It also allows Ron Lograsso the opportunity to do what he does best, concentrate on balls in the hole on the right side of the infield. He's quick on his feet, short of stature, and built close to the ground, attributes that allow him the luxury of doing something very few players in this league can do: dive to make plays. While there's no statistic kept for this, I'm convinced he leads the league in sprawling to the dirt, knocking the ball down, and completing a play somewhere.

He also has a great sense of humor. For example, he was

preparing to bat with me on deck to start an inning. At the time, he was also struggling with an early season slump. While we were standing there, I commented on his appearance, a mere two innings into the game.

"Look at you, already with your uniform all dirty, looking like a little Jose Altuve." Then with almost perfect timing, I add, "One of these days your productivity is going to catch up to your image." Some players might have told me mind my own damn business. Ron just laughed and, a few moments later, delivered a single to right field.

As the game progresses, however, it's the outfield that's taking on defensive water. The wind kicks up and fly balls begin turning into a deadly combination of strange base hits and balls bouncing off gloves or otherwise eluding defenders. But we shift folks around, successfully tighten up our play, and the game remains fairly close early on. The lead exchanges hands in the first few innings before our bats begin to come alive.

Meanwhile, our opponents this day, the Cubs, hit a defensive stride of their own and turn three double plays in the first four innings. Eventually our hard-hit balls begin eluding the same gloves that had been snagging them cleanly. Come the bottom of the ninth we take the field with a 10-run lead, which was a good thing given we also had about the same number of freshly pulled muscles at probably half the positions on the field. We literally limp our way to a 29-21 win. And I was among the limpiest.

How limpy were we? So limpy that even though I entered the game hobbled by slight pulls in both quads and my left groin, that still left me in an ambulatory enough state, compared to some of my teammates, to take on a pinch-running assignment in the early innings. Then in the 7th, my left hamstring gave way while beating out an infield hit. When the game ended, I was again grateful to have the next four-plus days devoid of any physical demands beyond walking as much or as little as I saw fit.

Over that time, and amid the balms and the stretching, I take a little time to get together with Martin Kurtz, father of three daughters, coach, and president of the Naples Girls Softball League. It doesn't take long to realize that baseball is woven into his family's heritage, much the same way as it has become a part of American life – over multiple generations. In the case of his family, that translates to over 130 years.

His great-grandfather played organized baseball in Indiana during the early 1900s. His grandfather, Arturo Fernandez Morell, excelled as an amateur player in Cuba. His 1943 Verdado Tennis Club baseball card lists as a $42 collectible online. Martin's wife played softball at the high school level. He played baseball throughout his youth and later school years with teams in Clewiston, FL, a small town on the edge of the Everglades, then on an intramural hardball team at Florida State. Now, in addition to heading up and coaching Naples Girls Softball, he continues to play recreational softball and, more recently, formed an adult hardball team.

With all that, the bulk of his focus these days is on the most recent family generation – three daughters ages 3, 7, and 10. It's a tradition he's happy being part of not only within his family, but the region in Florida where he's set down roots.

"There's an incredibly rich history of teams and leagues in this town," he says, immediately referencing a monument-like marker

on US 41 near the heart of the city. It reads: "Home of the World Champion Naples Braves and Naples Queens and Naples Gators. According to a 2019 article in the Naples Daily News, the glory years began in the early 1980s and continued into the early 2000s, a time in which the area was synonymous with girls fast-pitch softball excellence. Beginning in 1982, local teams won 18 World Series championships in Little League's various age brackets, including a run of eight in a row from 1989-96 in the girls senior division. Local high schools were also racking up state titles over the same period, especially in 1994 when three schools, Barron Collier, Naples, and St. John Neuman, all won their respective state divisions.

"The cool thing is that some of the girls who competed back then are moms today and coaching their own kids' teams," says Martin. They include Little League and Babe Ruth, along with about 120 young girls choosing Naples Girls Softball. "Our participation has held steady and is growing."

Most kids come to the league after playing co-ed tee ball. They're

Members of a Naples Girls Softball team participate in practice for their upcoming season.

divided into three groups ages 6, 7-8, and 9-10. He exposed his two eldest to soccer and tee ball and is happy both chose softball. Soccer at younger levels, he feels, is a lot of running around in groups that cluster around the ball. It's healthy but is short on skills instruction and teamwork.

"Softball seemed so much better for teaching teamwork and working with other kids. That's what we wanted our daughters to be a part of," he says, flashing a wry grin and some family bias when adding that he believes softball requires more skills. But he is fully serious when also noting that softball is more inclusive because it welcomes girls with a wider range of body types.

The thought seems to make sense both socially and athletically. I'm not familiar with many women ballplayers, but I chuckle imagining the likes of Babe Ruth, Yogi Berra, John Kruk, Prince Fielder, or, more recently, Bartolo Colon, C.C. Sabathia, or Vlad Guerrero Jr., even someone as big as Aaron Judge running around in shorts and a T-shirt kicking a soccer ball. I cringe at the image of any of them attempting a bicycle kick, even after endurance conditioning.

By Sunday, I'm feeling spry enough to easily get out and about. I decide to take a ride and watch Martin play with the Kraken, a local Men's Senior Baseball League team in their inaugural season. The Men's Senior Baseball League/Men's Adult Baseball League bills itself as the premier amateur baseball league for adults 18 and older. Founded in 1988 and based in Melville, NY, it boasts 325 local affiliates, 3,200 teams, and 45,000 members playing organized amateur baseball in local leagues throughout the country. The organization also holds 30 regional and 6 national tournaments. The league is separate from the National Adult Baseball Association (NABA) headquartered in Denver, which gives more than 25,000 players ages 18 and up the opportunity to compete in regulation baseball games in more than 125 leagues across 40 states.

The Kraken is one of two new MSBL teams that joined the

fledgling, six-team Collier County League in what is now its second year. The local league plays games on Sundays beginning in November and wraps up its playoffs by the end of April.

The Kraken's youngest player is 22. Their eldest is Bruce Ingleright, who tips the age-o-meter at 58. In between are Martin, 42, and player-manager Joe Pignatano, 35, a name that might be familiar to many old Brooklyn Dodgers and early L.A. Dodgers fans, and certainly fans of the original and early NY Mets teams. Joe's grandfather (also Joe Pignatano, but with a different middle name) was signed by his hometown Dodgers after an open tryout (yes they did that back then) at Ebbets Field in 1948. From there, he spent almost seven full seasons, interrupted by two years of military service, as a catcher in their farm system. Never approaching everyday, let alone star status, Pignatano's career did include several distinguishable, even memorable, moments.

He was behind the plate during the final five innings of the Brooklyn Dodgers' last home game at Ebbets Field against the Pittsburgh Pirates. He relieved starting catcher (and future Baseball Hall of Famer) Roy Campanella in the top of the fifth inning. Pitcher Danny McDevitt was tossing a shutout, and Pignatano did his part in helping him complete the task.

Before the Dodgers started their first campaign as the Los Angeles Dodgers in 1958, Campanella suffered paralyzing injuries in an automobile accident. John Roseboro replaced him as catcher and Pignatano became his backup, eventually playing a key role in LA's drive to the 1959 pennant. The Milwaukee Braves, winners of the two previous National League pennants and the 1957 World Series against the NY Yankees, finished the 1959 regular season in a tie with the Dodgers, forcing a three-game playoff.

Pignatano entered the second (and what proved to be final) game as a pinch runner in the ninth inning and replaced Roseboro at catcher in the top of the 10th after the Dodgers failed to score. Carl Furillo drove in Gil Hodges for the winning run in the bottom of the 12th inning, but not before Pignatano stroked a two-out single to keep the inning alive. He would soon earn his first World Series ring, as the Dodgers went on to win the fall classic in six games.

But after the dramatic finish for the pennant, the World Series that year is remembered more for a single, classic photograph of White Sox right fielder Al Smith than the Dodgers' six-game victory. The photograph garnered so much attention that it earned Smith a 2002 obituary in the New York Times. Smith was a solid ballplayer. But solid ballplayers didn't then and don't now routinely warrant lengthy obits in the Times. The headline read Al Smith, 73, Dies; Was Doused in Series. An extensive article that followed began:

Al Smith, the Chicago White Sox outfielder who became the hapless subject in one of baseball's most famous photographs when a fan spilled a cup of beer on him as Smith watched a home run sail over his head in the 1959 World Series, died Thursday at a hospital in Hammond, Ind. He was 73.

The cause was cardiac arrest after arterial surgery, his family said.

Smith played in the major leagues for 12 seasons, was twice an All-Star and was a starter with two American League pennant winners. But he was mostly remembered for one unfortunate moment.

The balance of the obituary talked mostly about the dousing, the fan, the photographer, and even the unusual camera he used (under development by NASA to record rocket-launch sequences). Smith's life and career were secondary to the moment. The article included an old quote from Smith stating he believed he must have signed 200,000 copies of the picture.

Pignatano, meanwhile, concluded his playing career in 1962 with the NY Mets as the only player to hit into a triple play in his final lifetime at bat. He remained with the team as a coach and won his second World Series ring in 1969 when he was bullpen coach for the so-called Miracle Mets. He earned far more attention in that

Roy Campanella and Joe Pignatano of the Brooklyn Dodgers talk catching in 1953. Pignatano's grandson (also Joe Pignatano), manager and member of the Kraken in southwest Florida, prepares to bat during a men's amateur baseball game in 2023.

role than would be expected because of a wild tomato plant he discovered growing in the Mets' Shea Stadium bullpen that same year.

Rather than pull the seedling, he cultivated it. The more it grew, the more attention the plant and he received from broadcasters Lindsey Nelson, Bob Murphy, and Hall of Famer Ralph Kiner. As the Mets continued toward their improbable miracle pennant drive and eventual World Series victory, Pignatano and the plant earned their own place in the national spotlight. He continued the tradition by planting a bullpen vegetable garden for luck each year during his tenure as a Mets coach, which ended in 1981. But thousands of Mets fans remember him to this day for his garden and friendly, engaging personality. Before his death in 2022, he also cultivated a love for baseball in his grandson, who, as these things go, came to be known in family circles as Little Joe.

At 35, and the father of a 6-month-old son, Little Joe's youth is filled with memories of life with his grandfather. He enjoyed the rare opportunity of learning the game from a big-league player. He also got to tag along with Grandpa at events such as old timers' games, meeting active and former players in various clubhouses, dugouts, and charity golf tournaments. "It was a great way to grow up," he says, standing near the Kraken dugout as the team prepares to take the field for their seventh game of the season.

It's like all dugouts, regardless of level. Gloves, bats, balls, pine tar, and other paraphernalia sit in racks or along the bench. Metal spikes click as players come and go, taking their places in the dugout and on the field. Sounds of laughter, encouragement, and, of course, frustration fill the air. There's the mandatory trash talk and razzing, especially between Joe and Martin, who also play on the same softball team, the former at third and the latter in the outfield. "I give him crap all the time," says Joe. "But it's all in fun. It's what we do."

Names on jerseys reflect an eclectic clan of 10 players, including the team's own version of the Alou family, brothers Peter and Dany Rivera. Add recent Cuban transplant Oscar Castellanos and the mix of players, languages and accents feels right to the eye and ear. It's all authentic baseball, down to the crack of the wooden bats. Yes, wooden bats. No pings on contact. Just the rich sound of ball on wooden barrel.

Baseball is their refuge and passion, but real-life distractions and jobs leave little or no time for team practice. They work things out as games and the season progress. For the Kraken, their downfall on this day is a spate of fourth-inning errors and mental lapses that give their opponent three additional outs. The misplays allow a handful of unearned runs to cross the plate and tip the score to 5-1 against them. At 22, pitcher Brandon Coraluzzo is the youngest and among the smaller players on the team. After the inning he tells Joe he's shot for the day. But during the half inning in the dugout he receives enough good-natured ribbing about his mental toughness to take the mound again.

When the Kraken are in the field Joe (the DH on this day) and I are left alone in the dugout to talk about the game that's going on and baseball in general. We agree that baseball, slow pitch softball

Brandon Coraluzzo pitching for the Kraken.

and everything in between are all variations of the same game. The skills required for each, with the exception of batting techniques, all translate regardless of the distance between bases and dimensions of the fields or player gender.

We swap stories, talk strategy, and exchange observations as the contest evolves. We watch Martin make two strong throws. On similar plays in two different innings, he gets to the ball, secures and transfers it to his right hand, gathers himself, and makes a hard, calculated throw from third to nip the runners. "That's why I put him there. He can field the ball and has a gun for an arm." The Kraken continue to shut down the opposition on a combination of gutsy pitching and solid fielding.

Then in the seventh inning they mount a serious rally with a walk, a soft liner to the outfield, and a long, soaring drive that looks at first to be a home run, but results in a double. They manage three runs, falling just short of tying the game when a runner is caught in no-man's land between third and home – another mental lapse. The game ends in a 1-2-3 bottom of the ninth and could have gone either way. Most players head out in a hurry, but a few hang around to pack up equipment and groom the infield. Overall, they end with an optimism that next week could go their way.

Encouraged by their energy and love of the game, the following morning I head out early for our Monday softball contest. I can bend and jog, but running hard is out of the question. After wrapping both legs and stretching out, I rate myself at about 75 percent capacity on defense, but require pinch runners on offense. On the upside, our team is beginning to gel defensively. We score early and often, then get lazy and sit on the lead. Our opposition, the Yankees, manage a rally in the fifth inning to draw within a few runs. We regain our focus and get on track again offensively while continuing to play pretty solid defense. The winning score is 17-11.

Wednesday, our first game in February, sets up to be a challenge. Tommy, arguably our best player, is in Tampa at a tournament with his other team, leaving us challenged to plug a big hole at shortstop. Things get a bit more questionable when Dave, one of our best hitters and regular starting pitcher, reveals he's had surgery and can only see out of one eye. There is, however, a silver lining. Sid Steinberger, a late-arriving newcomer to our league and team, turns out to be a fine glove and a decent bat. Defensively, he fits in perfectly at short and we don't seem to miss Tommy there. Even while scoring a season-low 14 runs, we earn a five-run victory.

Contributing to the bulk of our frustration was the truly stellar defensive play of an outfielder for the opposition Red Sox, Sharon Luebbert. After one of her three remarkable catches, I groaned in frustration. Bob Voss, a teammate standing nearby commented, "If we don't win this game, I won't live it down for a while."

"Why?" I asked. It was just another game to me. But for Bob, it turns out there were mitigating circumstances.

"She's my wife," he said, gesturing toward Sharon.

"She's your wife!? I hate your wife," cracked Gary Reizen, usually our quietest player.

There's some post-game chatter about moving Tommy, along with his arm and speed, to the outfield, and further shoring up what has become an improving situation there. We're already pretty good at scoring runs. Might we also improve dramatically on defense? While that reality exists, in this league, a sprain here and a pull there can always turn things quickly in the wrong direction.

For now though, our win coupled with an unexpected loss by the first-place Royals, puts us both at the top of the standings with identical 7-2 records. Days later, the Royals experience an even more unanticipated second straight loss. We also lose again and fail to capitalize on the Royals' cold spell, but tiebreakers make us winners of the first half of the season. While the overall standings don't reset for the second half, the honor isn't completely hollow, as it guarantees us one of the top two seeds come the March playoff tournament.

So, one month in, this journey with my glove is exceeding everything I had hoped it would be. There's some form of baseball at every turn. My legs, though heavily wrapped, seem to be on a steady mend. And my tired old glove isn't just staying in one piece, it's been resurrected with a supple quality that feels almost like an extension of my left hand, not just some addition or appendage to it.

Sure this over-60 league tucked away in southwest Florida amounts to significantly less than a hill of beans by any reasonable standard. But whether you're older than 20, 40, 60, 80 or even 90, winning is more fun than losing, regardless of the status or stakes.

CHAPTER 10

Stop Children! What's That Sound?

The crack of a baseball on a wooden bat – for those who love it, there's nothing audibly sweeter. For those who don't, may you live to hear the beauty in that sound. I heard it for the first time, really heard it, at Yankee Stadium in 1958, a few months before my 10th birthday.

My Dad was a working guy, a butcher; a solid union man who'd sometimes proudly refer to himself and his colleagues as meat cutters. Home, work, and recuperation from work didn't leave a lot of time or energy for play. So, it was a bit disorienting when he and I were alone together one summer Sunday after my mom had dropped us off at a subway station in the Bronx. We were going to a baseball game, a double header.

Actually, it was more than a "going" – it was a journey. First the car ride to the station; then the descent into the underground labyrinth of the New York City subway system – what an amazing world for a kid who was born in the Bronx, visited his grandparents and other family and friends there, but for most of his young life lived either just outside Toronto, Canada, or in the tamer suburbs of New York.

Guided by my father through this subterranean space of screeching steel wheels and shiny ceramic tiles bathed in an abundance of bright light, up the stairs we went onto the crowded city streets of the south Bronx adjacent to the Stadium. Finding our place in the gathering sea of fans, we flowed in hot, dense numbers, the likes of which I'd never seen or been a part of, past street vendors, souvenir stands, bars, toward the magnificent walls of the huge stadium with gates opened wide.

From a distance they looked like giant mouths swallowing up the masses. In fact, they were passageways to a magical world.

Strangers still towered all around, but the inside air of the ballpark's lower reaches felt cooler and welcoming. Up we went, past the signs for lower box and reserved seats; up past the mezzanine, passing images of men in uniform whose names I would one day soon utter with awe and reverence. Higher we went, toward our seats in the upper grandstand, my dad finally matching the section on our tickets with a sign on the wall. Up through the dark coolness, onto a ramp that opened to a crush of light so bright it overwhelmed my eyes.

When my irises adjusted, and pupils narrowed, my mind began the task of methodically wrapping itself around the visual spectacle. The greenest grass I could possibly imagine, surrounded by bleachers, field level seats and towering grandstands. All rose to meet the stadium's distinct ornate façade, the glistening whiteness of which seemed to match the few high hanging clouds drifting in the blue above. There it was before me, an almost incomprehensible panorama of colors and sights my senses could only begin to absorb. And those monuments in the far reaches of the outfield – were people buried there?

My head swiveled to take it all in, but the waves of astonishment had too much on me. My Dad settled us in our seats, tucked a bag of sandwiches under his, and pointed below to a cluster of men next to a netted frame I would come to know as a batting cage.

"See that one there, No. 7, that's Mickey Mantle. He won the Triple Crown," said my dad in a venerate tone I had never before heard from him.

"Wow," I said, having no idea what this Triple Crown thing was. But "wow" was all my developing 9-year-old mind could offer in response to this all-encompassing moment of visual astonishment and paternal bonding. Then, when my eyes had reached their limit, my ears took over.

Crack! My mind suddenly switched to audio. Crack! Then crack again!! I searched for the source of the sound, eyes settling on the figure with No. 7 on his back. The Triple Crown guy, Mantle, was swinging over, and over, and over again, each time launching balls on a line, on the ground, or high into the clean summer air – deep into the sky, past the infield dirt, over the green outfield grass, often far into the stands. Then he turned around and did it from the other side of the plate.

"See that," my father instructed. "He's a switch hitter." I had no idea what that was. But I surely wanted to be one.

Crack. … Crack. … Crack. That sound, that day, throughout that year and every year of my life since, it got to me then and gets to me now – in a way matched by music and exceeded only by love and friendship.

* * * *

It should come as no surprise then that on Super Bowl Sunday 2023, perhaps lured by the sound of ball on bat, I get up early and take in my second Kraken game. Don't get me wrong, I am not boycotting the big game. I simply find it hard to tolerate all the hype and analysis leading up to it, because – well, because it's just one game.

Sure it's a big game, a mega-game even. As an event, the day is as big as or bigger than any national holiday. Besides determining the champion of the NFL season, the halftime show and attention to in-game commercials place it at the zenith of the entertainment world. Globally the game itself may not be as big as soccer's FIFA World Cup, but as single day cultural event in America and elsewhere, nothing rivals it.

Still, it feels over hyped and oversold. Leading up to it, there are even commercials to promote the commercials, along with a show featuring commercials from past games. As a sporting event, it's always at risk of suffering under the weight of its own expectations, refereeing controversies, or other extenuating factors. Moreover, after two weeks of juiced-up prelude, the actual game doesn't begin until early evening. So even if you attend a morning religious service, and you're invited to the world's best game-day party, there's always time to kill before kickoff.

This day I choose the antithesis of the Super Bowl – an amateur baseball game with its occasional sweet-sounding crack of a baseball on a wooden bat.

There are almost as many players on the field as there are people in the stands. A cute, Cavalier King Charles Spaniel unknowingly competes with the game for fan attention. He wins for a while before running out of energy and settling down for a nap in the shade under a small stand of bleachers. Overall, there's an undeniably peaceful, wholesome hum to the late-morning/early afternoon activities – enhanced perhaps by little leaguers practicing on adjacent fields. I feel lucky to be here; grateful actually. Were I back north, filling the hours leading up to the Super Bowl could not possibly include going to a local park to watch amateur baseball. The game ends in another disappointing loss for the Kraken, but it accomplishes the job of filling a major chunk of time leading up to the big game.

With two hours till kickoff, I head out to join friends at a small gathering, which would be a stretch to call a party. By the time I arrive, remaining pre-game festivities and buildup to the opening coin toss include a shout out to first responders, a group of which surrounds Damar Hamlin. He appears to be in good health and enjoying the moment. The coming months will answer the questions around his ever again playing professional football. This being America, where personal branding has become a way of life, he has options. But the allure of competing at the highest professional level in any sport is strong. If he is medically cleared to play, his choice will no doubt be a most difficult one.

Meanwhile, the game is exciting, marred only by a correct, but questionable defensive holding call that gives the Kansas City Chiefs a late first down and allows them to take a knee and kill the clock for almost two minutes before attempting a winning field goal. How can a call be correct and questionable? It was not an egregious infraction. Many times, at the end of professional games, referees will "let them play." Be it basketball, football, or soccer, referees generally avoid calling late fouls and penalties unless they are flagrant. This one was not. What could have been an exciting final two minutes is instead a tedious exercise in watching seconds tick off the clock.

But that's enough talk about football, because with another season completed, it's time to focus on the fact that Major League pitchers and catchers have reported to their team facilities. Spring training is under way! And just as important for this fan and recreational player, the second half of Collier County's Naples Super 60 Softball League season is also about to begin.

For the Phillies, we begin again with a bye, so we get extra time to recover from any Super Bowl party overindulgences. Come Wednesday, following what was our worst offensive showing of the year the week before, we gather for a chance to avenge one of our earlier season losses and even our record against the Tigers. Their players include Ann Koenig. Halfway into the season her talents are being fully recognized. She's anchoring their infield from the shortstop position and batting high up in the order.

We come out fast on offense and make several sharp plays on defense, including two double plays, and mount an early 9-3 lead.

We're feeling quite good about ourselves – until we no longer can. Once again we slip into our Original Mets Mode, muffing grounders and not just dropping fly balls, but letting them bounce out of gloves as if the pockets were lined not with soft leather, but pinball machine cushions. And just when it looks like we're about to end the trend, one of our best outfielder races in to snare a medium depth, softly hit line drive only to overrun it, put on the brakes, and jump futilely in the air before sprawling onto the ground as the ball rolls past him to the centerfield fence.

By the time we get our defensive mojo back, it's the bottom of the 8th and we're trailing 16-9. With two out and no one on, we scratch out two runs. Our defensive play in the 9th keeps the deficit at 16-11. We go to bat in the bottom of the inning feeling hopeful, but not very confident. Then, with one out and no one on, the absurd occurs – make that the most bizarrely imaginable absurd. Everything we hit bounces off leather or finds a safe haven in the grass. Not just hard hit or well-struck balls, everything.

A short fly 10 feet from the infield becomes a hit when the middle-fielder turns, takes two stumbling steps and falls to the ground as if someone has tied his shoelaces together. A slow grounder rolls between short and third, before dribbling to the outfield after both players pull up at the same moment to let the other make the play. There are some legit hits too, but all that Original Mets Mode juice has now found its way to the opposition.

The near coup de grace comes on what resembles a Texas leaguer but fails to make it as far as Nebraska – metaphorically speaking of course.

Instead of an open swatch of outfield grass, this puny, bloopy projectile lands on a patch of infield dirt between the pitcher and second and first basemen, all of whom converge in the general vicinity of impact leaving no one to cover first base. That's followed by a legitimate final blow, a hard-hit, bases clearing liner that gives us a weird, but welcomed 17-16 come-from-behind Wednesday win.

There is something special to this victory, as well, but nothing significantly special. Remember, this is old folks' ball in a league where the stakes are about as low as they can be. Still, it reflects something exceptional about the human spirit. Sure, this is America, home to rugged individualism, or at least its mythical pursuit. However, the process of collectively contributing to an unlikely group accomplishment brings with it an exuberant sense of joy that goes far beyond the significance of the game.

We dug ourselves into a hole. But together, we came out of it. We depended on and encouraged each other to get there. Then we got there. Moreover, the opposing team's gloom was in no way the antithesis of our exuberance. Sure, there was a sense of bewilderment – what just happened to us here? But there also appeared to be something resembling a kind of unspoken appreciation that these kinds of turnarounds can occur when a group of vastly different people (and, man, are we an eclectic group) shares a common goal of any kind.

There seems to be an added sense of sincerity to the closing exchange between teams of "good game" high fives, fist bumps, and handshakes. Maybe there's also an intuitive understanding or hope that the quality of human spirit and potential demonstrated in today's silly softball game might also find its way to more meaningful theaters of human activity.

There's yet another benefit to this odd win. With our next game not till Monday, we can bask in our good fortune and once more take time to heal – because besides leading the league in wins, we continue to hold a clear edge in pulled muscles. It's increasingly more likely, it seems, that becoming a completely healthy team might not be in our stars.

Meanwhile, it's hard to believe that at this point we've completed more than half our season. Only eight games remain, one of them against the Red Sox, a matchup I've dubbed the family feud. It involves our Bob Voss and his wife, Sharon Luebbert, the Sox player who snuffed out several of our rallies with her exceptional outfield play the last time we met. When we got together in the weeks after that game they shared a bit of their history and what it's like to compete against one another.

As it turns out, both claim there's not much rivalry beyond minimal, in the moment, bragging rights. Both simply love each other, enjoy a shared, active life together, and also love playing the game. Except on the rare occasions when they find themselves on opposing teams, they're each other's biggest fans and best friends. They even agree she's the better player. Moreover, they also share my belief that baseball gloves are meant to be maintained, if not forever, for at least as long as oil and love allow. Both just had theirs restrung rather than replaced. But to be sure, Sharon's has been a bigger part of her life than Bob's has been in his.

"I've been playing since I was 4 years old," she says. When her sister's team was short a player, the coach (their mom) turned a blind eye to the 5-year-old age minimum. From those early days as an underage, kids-pitch player in Troy, Mo., just north of St. Louis, things kept moving forward. After that it was any form of ball she could find anytime she could find it, which turned out to be mostly fast-pitch softball – mainly as a pitcher or shortstop. And so it went, every year of her life right through high school. College ball was also on the table. "I had offers, but regretfully, I didn't go." Recreational and amateur options were mostly for slow pitch versions of the game. "I always wanted to find a fast-pitch team, but couldn't." Throughout her life and first marriage, even while raising four kids, she tried and mostly succeeded in finding leagues and time to play.

Bob's playing days have been, well, less consistent in comparison. He enjoyed baseball, played it some in Little League, but not a whole lot growing up or through high school in southern Illinois. He hung out and practiced with some players in college, but didn't choose or try to play anything organized. That changed later when he joined some recreational corporate teams during his working years. But with a job, wife, and two kids, that was enough for him.

Now, however, in addition to the Monday/Wednesday league, Sharon and Bob play in a Sunday morning pick-up game. When that wraps up, her focus will switch to regional and national play with a traveling, over-50 women's team based in Memphis.

They met at a divorce support group in 2015. Sharon was playing with a local league team at the time and, by 2017, her Memphis-based traveling team. "He'd come watch my tournaments," says Sharon.

"I was her biggest fan," says Bob. He means literally. They married later that year and settled down in suburban St. Louis until moving to their new southwest Florida home in fall 2022. That's when Bob decided to restring his glove and, together with Sharon, play in local pickup games. That led to participation in more organized play, including Collier County Super 60 Softball.

"I hadn't played at all in over 30 years," says Bob. "When we started out, it was Bob and Sharon. Now it's Sharon and Bob." He laughs.

That may or may not change as they continue playing in the years ahead. In the meantime, the Phillies have one more game against Sharon's Red Sox. It's ironic for me, a Yankees fan, that their Big League namesake in Boston has their "Bucky Bleepin' Dent" and "Aaron Bleepin' Boone" to wail about. After Sharon's first game against the Phillies, we too may have to find a suitable middle nickname for her. Bob may even join the nominating committee, because some memories are still especially fresh for him.

"I think her most incredible catch of the season was against me. If she didn't get it, it would have been my best hit of the year," he says.

"It was a good one," she agrees. "I had to race over and get behind the left-centerfielder and backhand it on the run." But there were at least three others against us, one of them in deep center on the warning track, another racing into a gap, and another charging

*Gear in tow,
Bob Voss and
Sharon Luebbert
arrive on game day
ready to play.*

in. Thankfully for Bob, none of those balls was hit by him.

"We would have scored at least five or six more runs that day if it wasn't for her," he says, still finding some solace in being able to claim victory.

"It wouldn't have mattered. I wouldn't have given him a hard time if we won," she says. Bob reacts with the subtlest of looks cast her way, accompanied by a tiny tilt of the head and slight squinting of the eyes that indicate he might think otherwise.

Over the next couple of days, I consider joining Bob and Sharon at the Sunday pickup game. After all, with the Super Bowl over, there's no more NFL to fill some of the weekend hours, and it would be good to get out and stay a bit active and engaged. But I've also come to enjoy attending Kraken games and watching live hardball. In addition to the sounds of the game, there's the slowing of time and appreciation for the moment that comes with exposure to the unfolding of the game. I think, too, that some of the players have grown comfortable with having me, my notebook, and camera around.

This week, when I arrive at the game, they're milling about the dugout resigned to the fact that they may not be able to play. The Rivera brothers are out of town, and a couple of other teammates have family conflicts. They have seven players but need eight to be allowed to start the game.

"Hey writer man," says Christian Cotto. "You want to suit up?" There are numerous reasons to just dismiss the overture as a crack from a 22-year-old unhappy at the thought of not being able to play. For one, I have no uniform to suit up into. I'm wearing shorts and a t-shirt, and their game is baseball, not restricted-slide softball. But as I look at these guys, it becomes clear that the invitation might be for real. They want to play and my body – all 74 years of it with its clearly wasting muscular structure, as sorry a specimen as it is – would give them eight players in a situation where it's seven men and you're out, eight and you can play.

Without really thinking it through, I hear myself saying, "If they'll allow it, I'll do it."

Manager Joe Pignatano walks off to confer with the opposing team and umpire. They look my way, smile a little (and maybe even laugh). Joe returns smiling too. "Let's do it. Where can you play?"

"Second base is what I know and it's the easiest throw. Does anyone have an extra shirt or old pair of uniform pants?" I ask, beginning to realize this is actually going to happen. They have nothing. All I have is my Dale Murphy RBG 36 glove and beat up, soft-spike golf shoes I converted for softball, as well as my game bag sitting in my trunk with knee supports, leg wraps, and ace bandages. I retrieve the bag, and without benefit of warming up, am all wrapped up and ready to go by the time my younger, better-dressed teammates have gone scoreless in the top of the opening inning.

The first thing I learn is that I can make the throw, all 90 feet of it from second to first. Better than just make it, there's enough zip on the ball to legitimize the effort. Joe, playing first today, seems pleasantly surprised. Compared to a softball, the baseball feels tiny in my hand, almost pea-like, and is swallowed up in the pocket of my glove. "Thus, the cliché of the baseball as pea," I say to myself, doing my best to be loose and relaxed in the situation.

Then it suddenly ceases to be a situation. It doesn't matter that I'm 30 to 50 years older than anyone else on the field, except for Bruce, the team's oldest roster player. At 50-plus he's a dead-fit natural athlete, doing his best to stay youthful for as long as he can. I remember those days and how muscles still responded to protein drinks and workouts. For the moment though, I realize all that matters is I'm playing freakin' baseball – organized, by-the-book, league-sanctioned, rules-regulated freakin' baseball. Sure, I'm playing in shorts. But that's okay as long as I don't have to slide, and I'd have to get on base to even consider having to do that.

Until then, these old legs and arms, riddled as they are with their share of sagging chicken skin, are in a crouch preparing to compete at whatever level of play they might have left in them. Not only, as Buck O'Neil says, does it bring me back, it all comes back to me – the chatter, the positioning with men on, working out with the shortstop who will hold the runner, who's covering on the steal – it's all still there, erupting at the surface like Old Faithful at an assisted living center.

Let's immediately put to rest any suspense about the outcome of the game. There are eight of us against 9 of them and one of us is ancient. The Kraken lose. But it's a beautiful loss on a glorious day in which that ridiculous notion that it's not whether you win or lose, but how you play the game, actually, for one day, makes absolute, total sense.

We play, for me at least, with magical joy. At the start, my goal is to represent to the point of not embarrassing myself, both in the field and at the plate. Notions of a game-winning hit are not on my radar and certainly not in any cards dealing in reality. These kids mostly throw in the 80s, and occasionally push 90. The only thing in my life that goes that fast is my car. Plus, they throw off speed and have decent breaking stuff.

The bats feel heavier than I recall them being 52 years ago or on any of the two or three occasions since that I think I recall being in a batting cage. Swinging with a weight in the on-deck circle helps a bit, but there's no changing the fact that I'm older, weaker, and lack anything resembling bat speed. Still, in my first at bat I get in my crouch and work the count full. I see a total of seven pitches, fouling one off the end of my bat to the right side that kind of clanks about 40 feet toward the first-base dugout.

I strike out swinging, but the pitcher needed a breaking ball to get me, and I just failed to hold off my swing for the walk. "Really! You need a 3-2 curve ball to get out an old guy?" I goad him on my way back to the bench.

Next time is a very similar at bat, except when the count goes full I look at a breaking ball and get a questionable called third-strike fastball. There's another difference. In between strikes I once more line a ball foul. While I'm again late on the swing, this time contact is squarely on the barrel of the bat, rocketing off the sweet spot wide of first base. It has that solid feel of a well-struck ball and makes that special sound: crack! I'm simply a little off on my bat speed and timing. Back on the bench I sense my team is beginning to take me seriously. I've made solid contact at the plate and recorded a clean 4-3 put out in the field.

In my final at bat, I decide if I turn around and bat lefty I might see the ball better. With the third baseman playing wide of the bag, I open up my stance and try to slap the ball toward him. I foul two off in his direction and again work the count full. This time I go down swinging on a high fastball that the umpire confirms he would have called a strike.

Meanwhile, in between those final two at bats, three good things happen in the field. The first comes with runners on first and second, and me shaded toward the bag to hold the runner. The batter hits a two-hopper up the middle that eludes the shortstop, but I'm able to backhand going to my right, just to the third base side of second. I make the transfer and flip the ball behind me while my momentum carries me toward leftfield. Would'a, could'a, should'a had him. All it would have taken was a slightly more accurate flip or a slightly better play by the shortstop.

The second good thing comes on a play when I couldn't quite get to the ball and field cleanly, but was able to knock it down and almost tag out the runner who had overrun second base. "Man, you have good hands," he said.

The third thing confirms the compliment. In the next half inning with one on and two out, the shortstop cleanly fields a sharp one-hopper, turns, and makes a snappy, chest-high throw to me covering second. I make a smooth pivot and transfer, followed by a perfect relay to first, completing the 6-4-3 double play. It also happens to be the Kraken's first of the season!

I didn't want this day to end, and it didn't for a while. Four of the players with no family obligations decide to go to a local marina bar. The plan is to have a couple of drinks and then go to a local symphony performance – dressed as we are – so starting pitcher Brandon Coraluzzo can keep a promise to attend that he had made to a flutist friend. We shift our commitment when first baseman Phil Viar, who arrived to the game around the seventh inning after attending his daughter's equestrian competition, counters with an offer to meet us at the marina on his boat and take us out to Key Wade for an afternoon of swimming and partying.

Max Troiano, the Kraken's diminutive and perhaps most complete all-around player, works for Phil and is assigned to get us to the pick-up point. It turns out that Max gets confused quite easily after a certain amount of alcohol consumption. We make it to neither the concert nor the boat. But none of that seems to matter as we all happily make it to the end of the afternoon and safely home. That includes Christian Cotto, the starting catcher and relief pitcher, who remains convinced that if our waitress weren't working a double shift, she would be going to dinner with him. Ahh youth – sometimes it isn't wasted on the young.

I, along with several members of the Kraken, enjoy a post-game celebration of my brief, surprise return to regulation baseball. From left: John Pearson, Brandon Coraluzzo, Max Troiano, myself, and Christian Cotto.

CHAPTER 11

Monday, Monday

The following morning, it's back to softball as usual with the Phillies. The usual, however, is beginning to take on an alarming tendency. We again get off to a big lead via solid hitting and sharp defense before slipping into a bit of a fog. This day, however, our funk is less Original Mets and more zombie stupor. It begins in our top of the third with no one out and a runner on second who decides it's a good idea to go to third base on a sharp ground ball fielded cleanly by the shortstop. The throw beats him by a time zone.

It goes on like that both defensively and offensively for three more innings. The day is sunny and clear, but between the ears and reflected in everything we do, it's all London foggy. Meanwhile, things are coming up sunshine and roses for the Cardinals, our opponent on this weird day. By the end of the sixth we're trailing by two runs. At that point, if forced to make a wager who would win, I would have bet on the Cardinals. Yet somehow, we take a two run, 24-22 lead to the top of the ninth.

How weird do things get? Well, we wind up scoring 17 runs to go ahead 41-22, a score that exceeds the flip-numeral scoreboard limit of 39. It's not like we were pounding out hit after hit. Their pitchers had been having trouble throwing strikes all day. For some reason we just decided to stop swinging at pitches that were balls. And when they did throw strikes, we hit them hard.

Come Wednesday, we could have used some of those runs. Our opponent is the Royals, the team we were rained out against in the first half of the season. They're one of the more fundamentally sound teams in the league.

Both clubs play fairly sharp ball, but we continue to be plagued by mental lapses when focus is most required. The game tips back and forth. In the seventh, we run into an out at third base, the first of the inning. Ill-advised base-running resulting in outs (too often at third base) is an occasionally haunting flaw we just can't seem to shake.

"Why does this kind of crap happen at just the wrong time?" asks a frustrated teammate.

"When is the right time for that crap?" I ask back.

"Good point," he says shaking his head.

Frustration carries over into the top of the ninth. With the score tied at 14, we're scheduled to send the bottom five batters in our order to the plate. Usually a relatively patient team, as our big ninth inning on Monday indicates, the first three batters offer at the first pitch they see, each making a one-swing out. It's a frightening display of a total lack of situational awareness. A three-pitch half inning in this league is almost unheard of. Yet we do it in a most crucial situation.

After wiggling out of a bases-loaded jam in the bottom of the ninth, things momentarily look hopeful. But starting with a "ghost runner" on second in the top of the 10th, we revert once more to critical lapses in fundamentals when the runner fails to advance on a long, arching, weak throw to first that just manages to nip the batter. We threaten by loading the bases with two outs but fail to capitalize. The runner left on third would have scored easily had he advanced when he should have. Outplayed in a very competitive matchup, we lose in the bottom half of the 10th to a team that performed a little better than we did because they played a whole helluva lot smarter.

The worst part about a Wednesday loss is we must wait until Monday to play again. Compounded by the way we lost will make the wait even longer. Or so I felt the afternoon following the game. Come Thursday, my attitude shifts back to "ain't life grand!" I have four glorious days to fill with warm weather activities, free of the blizzards, ice storms, and winter's chilling cold back north. The news reminds me there's war, famine, poverty, and all kinds of real human pain in the world. Instead of lamenting a poorly played game and a silly, small-stakes loss, I should be looking for a suitable charity to which I can donate.

My thoughts revert to the unexpected joy of playing with the Kraken a few days before, and the opportunity to watch them play, maybe even win come Sunday. I recall all the good things of the week, including pizza with my friend Bobby Bohara, a teammate from 2019 now shelved by illness. He's the one player from that Orioles team I've kept in touch with over the years. Following his diagnosis, Bobby donated all his softball equipment, but continues his connection with the league. When doctor appointments don't create a conflict, he keeps the scorebook for a team managed by one of his friends. We laugh, reminisce, and share stories while his wife, Linda, is kind enough to pick up the pizza. My donation food-wise to the evening is a key lime pie.

We eat, laugh, and carry on for several hours, after which I decide to take a slight detour on the way back to my apartment and watch a few innings of a Naples Girls Softball League scrimmage. Talk about joy! Their unbridled enthusiasm and appetite for playing and learning the game is unlike anything I've ever seen. Players take on the role of both team and cheerleading crew. One team's coach, Jessica Buther, is a former Little League Softball World Series champion. Now a 35-year-old mother of two girls and a boy, she's relishing the opportunity to coach one of her own daughters.

"I love it. I absolutely love it," she says. Her coaching philosophy involves the push to develop better players, while employing a balance of passion and compassion. She wants to tap her own history as child, college player, and woman athlete to help her young players understand the ups and downs of learning how to compete.

"It's OK. You're not going to get a hit all the time. You just gotta take these emotions and practice harder," she says. It's a tightrope all athletes walk, the balance of trying to perfect one's skills with the knowledge of knowing there is no such thing as perfect play.

Some of her philosophy percolates in the dugout while the team is batting. The cheering and support is loud, energetic, spontaneous, and contagious, occasionally taking a unified form where one leads and the others respond in a chant-like cadence that resembles what one might associate with a marching platoon.

Leader: Who's that player at the plate? Others in unison: Who's that player at the plate?

Leader: She's the best in all the state! Others: She's the best in all the state!

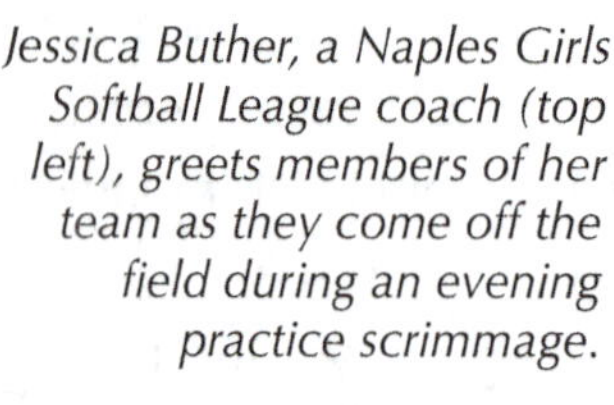

Jessica Buther, a Naples Girls Softball League coach (top left), greets members of her team as they come off the field during an evening practice scrimmage.

Leader: She can run and she can slide! Others: She can run and she can slide!

Leader: Best of all she's on our side! Others: Best of all she's on our side!

On the field, pitchers, hitters and position players engage in spirited play as several coaches shout direction or quietly take individuals aside for instruction. Activity and dialogue are upbeat and constant. The team huddles between innings and shouts "defense" in unison before transitioning to their positions. On a scale of 1 to 10, their enthusiasm would bury the needle of any measuring device real or imagined. In the days that follow, I find myself thinking about the joy these young women take in learning the game.

Individually, they listen intently when Jessica or one of her assistants instructs them in the fundamentals: how to get the bat in proper position; how to initiate a swing that engages the hips and larger muscles; the importance of relaxing between pitches; when to take an extra base – the players have a thirst for learning and doing things the right way. Not only do they want to participate, but they're also hungry to compete.

The other three fields of the complex are occupied by boys Little League teams. My son came up through the Little League ranks, and what I see here on this day is pretty much consistent with what I saw then. I take in the scene of all these boys and girls playing the game I grew up loving, and can't help but think that the future is bright for fans and players alike.

As the days roll ahead toward Monday, I make mental plans for the weekend: Spend Saturday morning in town, walk to the Gulf of Mexico, hit my favorite coffee shop, and maybe take in a Kraken game. I check almost every item off the list by Sunday morning, which is when the Kraken play. They're able to field a full complement of players, but fall into their usual pattern of issuing too many walks compounded by errors in the field.

This week, however, walks aren't quite as numerous and they cut down on their number of miscues. Coupled with livelier bats on offense and some stellar plays on defense, they keep the game relatively close. After jumping out to a 1-0 lead, they fall behind 3-1 in the top of the second. The game stays within reach, with each team putting runs on the board here and there, before their opponents stretch it to 9-5 in the top of the seventh. The Kraken fail to score in their half of the inning, but also hold the deficit at four runs going into the bottom of the eighth, which will be the last of it because of a three-hour time restriction on games.

The key hit comes on a shot back to the pitcher by Max Troiano, one of the 20-something players on the team whose game is all about speed, hustle, and scrappiness. He dives at anything within reach in the outfield, and more often than not makes the plays. His uniform is always dirty early and just gets dirtier as innings progress. His enthusiasm is contagious, his body always at risk. He shows up for every game and comes ready to play. If the league required

Max Troiano finds himself once again in search of a good dry cleaner after a head-first slide into home during a close Kraken game.

nicknames, Max "the Generator" Troiano would have to be in the running. The Energizer would work too, but that's already taken by a pink mechanical rabbit. Maybe Pigpen because of the uniform – but I digress.

The hard-hit liner caroms off the pitcher's glove. The race is on as the pitcher scrambles to retrieve it, and Max bursts off toward first. With the shortstop also breaking toward the ball, there's an instant sense of panic. The scramble continues as everyone knows Max is in after-jet mode and creating a dusty blur running down the line. He beats the throw, and from there things begin to unravel for the other team. Suddenly, it's the opposition's pitcher who can't find the plate. Walk by walk, with an occasional hit thrown in, the Kraken score five runs to earn the win.

After so many disappointments and frustrating losses, it's clearly a big victory for a group of guys I've come to know a bit and enjoy watching play. Having been tapped for emergency service the week before, I feel less like a 74-year-old wrinkly mascot and more like the injured player on the club who still shows up for the game and roots from the bench. This rag-tag bunch of merry amateurs have come to be a part of my weekly routine, and I can't help but feel fortunate for the opportunity to feel connected to them.

Moreover, while Max may have had the key hit in the inning, the biggest hit, for an entirely different reason, belonged to Bruce Ingleright, who, at 58 is the eldest member of the team. Despite the age difference, the two have a lot in common, with the exception of speed. Max can motor and Bruce's lack of speed is the anchor he's dragged behind him most of his playing days. Regardless, Bruce has always been a hitter and still can hit the ball really, really hard.

He also flashes the kind of bat speed you know is quick even without measuring. When he squares the ball up, the crack sounds, as the phrase goes, a bit different. But the balls he's hit square seem always to be at somebody or they're run down and turned into outs. His 0 for 11 slump ends with a hit that prompts the entire

*Bruce Ingleright connects on a key hit during
a come-from-behind Kraken win.*

Kraken team, conscious of his mounting frustration, to erupt in ear-pounding cheers of support.

"I started playing when I was 4 years old," says Bruce, who took to pitching as well as hitting. "From age 5 to 17, nobody was touching my fastball." During his youth he played whenever and wherever possible, including various summer and Connie Mack leagues. He also made several trips to baseball instructional camps in Fort Lauderdale where he could learn from the various pro players on staff. "I really focused in on technique."

By his early teens he was all-in on a possible career in baseball and was an all-around star athlete. He hit a trifecta of sorts by making his Valley Forge High School baseball, basketball, and football varsity teams his sophomore year in Parma, Ohio. "Nobody had done that in 20 years," says Bruce. He gave up basketball and football his junior year to focus on pitching. By the late 1980s his future was looking good enough to earn an invitation to the Olympic trials. But things suddenly hit an insurmountable roadblock. "My fastball topped out in the upper 80s. I might occasionally hit 90, but that was it."

In a world where 95 mph was the new 90, and no big-league scouts or teams were interested in developing finesse pitchers, he focused on hitting and converting to position play. Based near Cleveland, he hooked up with any amateur team he could find, including one in a multi-tiered league sponsored by the Cleveland Plain Dealer, where he reached AAA, their highest classification.

With a strong arm, soft hands, and quick first-step reflexes, he focused on third base. His hitting really came around as well. But the years were piling up. He was on the wrong side of 25 when he had a great year both defensively and offensively. "The constant strength and flexibility training was paying off."

Now a salesman by trade, in 1983 he tapped those skills, called in some chits, worked his contacts, and convinced the Cleveland Indians farm system to give him a spot in a group tryout. Throwing, running, and hitting were the focus — in that order.

When they put the stop watch on him, his lack of speed killed the dream.

"They never even watched me hit," he says, a twinge of sadness persisting in his voice to this day.

From then on, it was whatever form of softball was available. He just kept playing and loving the competition. Then, in 2017, he got a call from a high school pal encouraging him to play in a Cleveland area hardball league. It didn't take much convincing. He signed up and jumped right back into the groove on 45- and 53-plus teams. Since then, it's been all the hardball he can eat. When the Kraken season ends, he'll head north and reboot the cycle again.

He's a baseball junkie," says his wife, Teri, who doesn't mind supporting his habit. "He just loves to play."

"He always has," chimes in Toni, his 94-year-old mother. She laughs, smiles, and offers up an approving nod from a mom who still ventures out when she can to watch her boy play the game he can't help but love.

Watching him and Max play their hearts out for the love of it, one can't help but think that if they could just somehow morph their bodies into a single, younger one, the result would resemble something akin to Dustin Pedroia, the four-time All Star second baseman who played for the Boston Red Sox from 2006-19.

CHAPTER 12

The Name Game

With six games left in our regular season, I've begun taking my Rawlings Dale Murphy RBG 36 glove for granted. I guess that makes sense. Isn't that what we humans tend to do in our relationships – take our partner for granted? And there's no doubt that my glove has been both partner and catalyst in this whole process.

I decide to name it. Maybe even talk to it a bit. You know, like Tom Hanks did with Wilson in Cast Away. Not to the extent he did, of course. I'm not stranded on a remote, desert island. There are other people to talk with in my life – though there was that day in the basement a few months back I thought I heard it talking to me.

But what shall I name it? Clearly, it can't be Rawlings. That works for a brand, but on a personal level it seems more suitable for an English butler. Moreover, it would be an act derivative to the point of being inexcusable – Wilson/Rawlings.

Next I consider the number 36. But that sounds like a name more appropriate for a legendary steam-powered locomotive than a baseball glove. You know, as in "Old 36, whistle blowing in the night, moving freight from Macon to Memphis." Sing it Johnny, sing it. So forget the numbers.

What about the letters then? RBG, which I noted earlier are

shared by the late Supreme Court Justice Ruth Bader Ginsburg. So, maybe Ruth or Ruthie? In today's social climate there is no telling who I might offend for any number of reasons by going that route. Ginsburg? Nah. It's a baseball glove, not a beat poet or a New York delicatessen.

Bader?

Bader!!

Now this might have some potential. Two syllables, and it's also the last name of current Yankees centerfielder Harrison Bader! What's more, he grew up in Bronxville, the same New York City suburb in which I spent most of my own youth. Bader it is!

I understand that most people might find it a bit loony, or at least nonsensical, for an adult to name their glove with the intention of talking to it, however briefly or infrequently. To those people I would say: You just don't get it. And if you don't believe me, go ask Mike Gallego. You remember him, the guy who ran back into a shaking Candlestick Park to retrieve (or maybe in his mind rescue) his beloved and trusted glove during an earthquake.

How rational are most things we do as human beings anyway? The one that always got me as a kid was building the atom bomb. I had a paper route at a time when the Soviet Union and the U.S. were cranking out nuclear weapons like Hershey's was producing chocolate bars. The headlines about the arms race and the size of the bombs both countries were testing were as terrifying as the potential for a nuclear holocaust was possible. I remember asking myself why anyone in their right mind would take what was then thought to be the smallest particle of matter and split it with the intent of blowing other, larger pieces of matter into oblivion?

The question truly perplexed my developing young mind. Who would do such a thing? Why, human beings would, of course. What's more, they'd compete against each other to do it better. As I see it, then, naming a baseball glove doesn't rank very high on any list of irrational human behavior.

Now, with the name settled, my legs continuing on the mend, it's on with the games. The first for us is on Monday, Feb. 27, against the Cubs. We both enter the game with 2-1 second-half-of-the-season records, so as these things go, it's a game with some significance. As it progresses, we exchange the lead, with both teams falling victim to an inning each of bungled defensive play. The game remains relatively close, with no one gaining more than a two-run advantage. It stays that way going into the ninth. In the top half our bats wake up a bit and we take the field with a 16-11 lead. They threaten, but we make plays when we have to, and the game ends in a five-run Phillies victory.

In the process, I learn a bit about the art of talking to one's glove. Unlike Tom Hanks' conversations with Wilson, it isn't always necessary to address a glove by its given name or carry on lengthy conversations. We are not best friends or constant companions. The act of naming a glove is more an acknowledgment of the intimate connection to purpose and process the joining together of player and glove represents.

By our next game, I've got it down to a simple act of recognition. A silent "let's do this" directed to the soft extension of leather on my left hand as we take the field for our Wednesday game against the Yankees is all that's required. Just a simple act to acknowledge the connection of spirit between an animate being and what any uninformed outsider might believe to be a soulless object.

The game is initially close. Both sides play fairly tight defense and have no trouble producing runs on offense. It's also a milestone of sorts – we've made it to March. Winter is almost behind us. Spring, the season of hope, will soon be in the air. And so it is with a somewhat similar sense of elusive hope that I take off in pursuit of a short, looping pop fly to centerfield in the bottom of the eighth inning.

The play begins with one out and runners on first and third with us nursing a slim 18-16 lead. The ball appears to be a certain hit, but off I run anyway, head down, arms pumping, ever the dreamer, toward an approximate point where I believe it will land. I look up and, wouldn't you know it, I guessed correctly. There, about 15 feet above my head and dropping fast is the bright yellow object of my pursuit.

At this point two more things must happen: one, I have to get to the ball; two, I have to catch it. Moreover, both acts must occur in the combined span of something less than a second. And if they do, it would be one helluva catch. I begin to stumble as I reach out toward the ball. It hits Bader halfway up the webbing. Leather wraps around leather. I continue stumbling, and as I do, reach for the partially exposed ball, transfer it to my right hand and, falling to the ground, flip it over my head back in the general direction of second base.

When I get to my knees and turn back toward the infield, Tommy already has the ball and is looking to make a play on one of the runners. Both get back to their bases safely, but neither scores. The next play is a routine out that ends the threat. As for the catch, it's the highlight of my season and will remain so. Even if I were to miraculously summon up some kind of Ruthian power and hit a grand slam over the centerfield fence in the bottom of the ninth to win the championship (that would be miraculous for sure) it wouldn't top the rush of making this catch. It feels that good!

We put up six runs in the top of the ninth and take the field in the bottom of the inning with a 24-16 lead. The game ends on a hard one-hopper to Tommy, who fields it cleanly in the hole at shortstop and makes a strong, accurate toss to me at second for the final out. I hold onto the ball for a keepsake, placing it in Bader's pocket and securing ball and glove in my gear bag.

It's part of the umpiring routine to secure the two game balls at the end of every game. The good ones go back into play, the rest into the batting practice buckets. As I run off the field, there's a hunt for the one I've kept, the same one that I had caught in the previous inning.

"I don't think Phil's giving it back," says Tommy. He's right, of course.

* * * *

This is the third season I've seen Tommy play. The first was in 2017, my initial year in the league and his fifth. He was a top-flight player then and remains one now at 71. He might be a step slower and his throwing motion a tad more restricted than before, the expected result of making one's way deeper into retirement. However, he remains dead fit, wiry, muscular, and devoid of any apparent body fat.

He goes to the plate expecting a hit every time. He bats sans cap for the most part, long, thick locks hanging almost to the shoulders with no apparent graying. My presumption was that he must color it. I finally asked him about it once and he good-naturedly bent over, said something about the effects of sunshine and chlorine, and offered his roots up for proof to the contrary.

"See, there's gray in there," he laughed, parting the strands with his fingers. He's right; there's some, but so little that one might still think he's found some variation of the fountain of youth in his Florida backyard.

A native and former long-time resident of northern Michigan, Tommy runs hard, plays hard and is highly competitive. When he hits the ball, he takes off from the batter's box, legs churning, hair flowing, lacking any intention of stopping until he absolutely must, or if he makes an out. When he does make an out, he thinks he should have had a hit. If he hits a single, he reacts as if it should have been a double. Doubles should be triples and … Well, you get the idea. Watching him, one can't help but think this guy started playing the game before he could walk, was an obsessed star growing up, and will continue playing until he can no longer stand without a cane.

And if you thought that – well you know what they say happens when you assume. In this case, you'd be right on one of three assumptions. Tommy will likely not stop playing until he can no longer walk without support.

However, the astonishing thing is that he never played baseball growing up, and hardly played any form of the game until after he retired 10 years ago. But when the bug finally bit him, he couldn't stop scratching the itch, and he couldn't stop itching to play better, and better, and better.

"I was always competitive, but always found other outlets," says Tommy. At one point he was a runner and worked hard at it, competing in 10Ks for the most part as a member of various running clubs. "I never broke 40 minutes but could average just under seven minutes for a mile. That's pretty good, but genetically, I just wasn't constructed to be any faster."

When he arrived in southwest Florida, he looked around for physical activities to get involved in. "I noticed there were a lot of softball leagues and decided to give it a shot." Once he made the decision, he took it very seriously, working hard in the gym and even harder to become the best player he could possibly be.

Tommy Turton takes one of his typical all-or-nothing swings.

Now when the season is in full swing he plays in two leagues, four days a week, participates in batting and fielding practice with younger players on weekends, and regularly plays in travel team tournaments.

"I like working out with the younger kids. They can really hit the ball hard and high. When you shag their long fly balls, it helps keep your depth perception sharp," he says.

There may be a couple of players in our league who are a little faster, throw a little stronger, move a bit better in the field, or hit with more power, but they don't play harder. All are considerably younger, and certainly none of them has more fun competing. What's more, his youthful enthusiasm is contagious and enhances the joy of playing alongside him.

* * * *

Our win against the Yankees is our 10th of the season against four losses, and puts us in a tie for first place in the second-half standings with a 4-1 record, which matches the Red Sox, our next opponent. Although we beat them 17-11 in our first encounter, it was a close game until the end. Much of that was due to the incredible defense by Sharon Luebbert. Her husband, as you may recall, is Bob Voss, one of our outfielders. So bragging rights, in a game we've dubbed The Family Feud, are on the line.

Circumstances dictate the game be played at a different location, as the fields at Collier Park will be taken up by a two-week girls softball tournament. The shift to Veterans Park requires us to share fields with additional teams, creating a scenario in which teams playing in late games don't get to work out on the field or take batting practice. This game, however, is an early one.

We immediately get off to a great start defensively, with two pop outs to the infield on the first two pitches. But it doesn't last long. The Sox unleash a barrage of clutch hitting and solid base running around a couple of walks. The result: A two-out, three-run rally. We make two quick outs as well in the bottom of the inning, but then also respond with two runs of our own.

Back on the field, we again play solid defense, which to my delight is something I've begun observing about our team a bit more of late. As bodies get a little healthier, we have more flexibility in positioning players and the results are beginning to be increasingly positive. We hold them scoreless and take a 4-3 lead into the third inning. From then on, we manage a modest nine additional runs for the entire game. But that defense I've been talking about is having a great day. Over the next six innings, as we continue to play well in the field, nothing but zeros go up on their side of the scoreboard.

Our outfielders are getting to balls, backing each other up, and the only plays that don't go our way are the occasional bleeder or ball lost in the sun of a very high, bright Florida sky. The infield is similarly solid. Only two throws go offline, along with one dropped ball at first base. We field most balls cleanly and ones we don't handle cleanly are knocked down with time to make force plays. We go into the final inning ahead by what feels like a very comfortable 13-3 margin. The Sox manage to get two base runners, but there are two outs when a hard, sinking line drive heads toward shallow left centerfield.

Angelo Vitale, our left fielder has missed several games this year with strained calf muscles in both legs. He's been feeling better of late but has not run at full speed. He breaks into a hard sprint and closes ground quickly, then dives for the ball. The results initially look ugly. When he rolls over, his left arm bends at a weird angle and the ball leaks out of his glove onto the grass. I wait for a scream and an outcome no better than a dislocated shoulder.

The guy with fragile calves, though, must have bones of rubber and elastic rotator cuffs. He grabs the ball sitting next to him on the ground and flips it to Tommy, who runs it back to the infield. The

Sox load the bases, but the play occurs so quickly that the runner from second holds at third. The next batter hits a hard shot toward right field. Second baseman Ron Lograsso knocks it down, finds it in the dirt, and flips it to second for the final out.

A combination of defense and a minimal number of walks issued by Dave Smith, our pitcher, result in the Red Sox failing to score for eight consecutive innings! I may be playing on the Phillies in over-60 softball, but in real life I'm a diehard Yankees fan. So, it doesn't matter that the Red Sox we beat this day are also a bunch of older players, because it's a great day anytime any team bearing that name is shut out for eight straight innings. That it happens in a high-scoring form of softball makes it less meaningful, but no less sweet. Moreover, Bob can head home knowing he won the most recent matchup with Sharon and retains his household claim to team superiority.

With three games remaining in our regular season, our second half record is 5-1, giving us a one game lead over the Red Sox, Dodgers, Royals, and Cubs. Our overall record improves to 11-4, for a one-game advantage on the Royals in the cumulative standings. Next up are the Orioles, who handed us another of our first-half losses. The game is a late start, giving us time for doughnuts, coffee, and socializing beforehand, but no batting practice.

I spend some of the pregame chat time with the two oldest players on our team, Jim Heckel, 82, and Jim Neuser, 89. Jim H. came into the season nursing a bad back that will require surgery. He tried to play early on before deciding it wasn't worth risking further damage. Moreover, his back condition doesn't allow him to freely swing a bat.

But he shows up to every game, coaches third base, and musters up moral support for the rest of us. He's that kind of "I'll do what I can" teammate who helps make a team better. Everyone welcomes his quiet, supportive presence.

Jim Neuser's presence also is welcome. But it's anything but quiet. Nine months shy of his 90th birthday, he's what my late Aunt Jo used to call a chatterbox. He rambles and rambles about anything and everything. He talks about his seven kids. He talks about his 20 grandkids. He talks about his 22 great-grandchildren. He talks about the replacement surgery scars on both his knees and how well the new ones work. He talks about the hotel he bought in Acapulco that could have made a fortune but cost him his shirt.

He'll talk about what it's like to be 89, and then about what it was like when he was a kid. He'll talk about how he can't hit the ball like he used to, and about how hard he could hit it when he was younger… You get it. Jim likes to talk.

His mind is sharp and so is his wit. One might question the quality of his wittiness, but he's still quick with a retort. He'd probably offer up even more quips, but his hearing is so poor he misses many opportunities.

The most important qualities he brings to the team are enthusiasm, a self-deprecating sense of humor, and being a walking, talking reminder that life can be full, so long as it's approached with an engaging mind, gratitude, and the joy in just being present. He

The Phillies' two elder statesmen, Jim Neuser (left) and Jim Heckel.

also knows how to work the pitcher for a walk and can surprise everyone, including himself, with an occasional hit. And when he does, he'll talk about it until you make him stop. When he's catching, he talks to opposing batters. Perhaps his greatest contribution on the field is how much he distracts them.

He's also at his most confounding when playing catcher, where he has trouble keeping anything in his glove except his left hand. During warm-ups, he can catch and throw with nary a drop. During the game, however, something in his still-sharp mind clicks off and, in the process, seems to wrap his glove in cellophane. Instead of catching the ball, he finds new ways to juggle it. But that's when his sense of humor kicks in and he's at his self-deprecating best.

There's no escaping that the key to maximizing having fun in this league is accepting that as we get older, our skills will continue to erode. Games are going to be high scoring not only because we can hit, but also because we randomly can misplay almost any kind of fielding opportunity. Jim not only gets that, but shows the rest of us how to accept it.

When the late game finally starts, it's a good one that indicates, as the season is winding down toward the playoffs, our defense is gelling while our offense remains in gear for the most part. Early on, while scoring is modest for both sides, we manage to put together a 5-3 lead after three innings. Each team scores occasionally through the middle frames, until we explode for six runs in the bottom of the eighth and carry a seven-run lead into the ninth. They threaten, but we again do all the right things on defense. The last out is a hard-hit ball to second base that Ron Lograsso dives for and knocks down. The move adds more dirt to an already dirty uniform before he scrambles to his knees and throws to second for the force play. Final score: Phillies 18, Orioles 11.

Our overall record now stands at 12-4 with two games remaining in the regular season. The first is against the Cardinals, a team that, despite a poor record, managed to beat us in our first meeting. Our final opponent will be the Royals, another team we lost to previously and finished ahead of by a game in the first half standings. We also lead them by a game in both the cumulative and second-half standings. However, there are very few scenarios under which our final matchup won't be essential to resolving not only the second-half standings, but the overall Season Championship.

As is the case every week, I must fill almost five full days between the last out of our Wednesday game and Monday when we resume play. There's a line in a Townes Van Zandt song To Live is to Fly that claims, "Living's mostly wasting time and I waste my share of mine." Most of my attention over these spans involves activities related to writing, grocery shopping, and perfecting the art of "mostly wasting time." Florida can be a fine, warm escape from winter's grip, but there's a limit to my sun worshiping capacity.

Additionally, most of the golf courses, at least in this area, are overpriced and overplayed during what natives refer to as "the season" – that roughly three-month span when snowbirds like me migrate and overpopulate the roads, restaurants, and other popular landing grounds. After a little more than two months of my own migration, and with no members of a personal flock with whom to fly about, I've begun to run out of appealing choices on my menu of time-consuming options.

I continue to attend Kraken games on Sundays, but they're in the midst of a downward spiral. After their comeback win of several weeks ago, they were almost no-hit the next time out. This week they came back mid-game to tie the score at 3-3, but reverted to giving up too many walks and committing destructive errors in key situations.

Big league spring training camps are plentiful, but I've avoided them because you never know what team you're going to see if you attend a Grapefruit League game – something resembling the actual club, or a lineup filled mostly with minor leaguers and free agents desperately trying to hook up with a team. This year the situation is complicated by the World Baseball Classic, a global tournament of the best players from countries around the world competing in a field of 20 national teams. Although it hasn't caught my full attention, bracket play gets under way this week, and I've begun to check it out.

The World Baseball Classic represents the coming together of several global organizations (including the International Baseball Federation and the World Baseball Softball Confederation in association with Major League Baseball and the Major League Baseball Players Association, along with a number of other leagues) and players associations around the world. With the aim of promoting the game globally, the Classic came into being after the 2005 International Olympic Committee's decision to remove baseball as an Olympic sport.

Japan won the first two competitions in 2006 and 2009. Held every three years at that point, both tournaments ranked among the highest-rated sporting events in Japanese television history. Organizers have since continued to tweak the format and selection process. Currently modeled after the FIFA World Cup, 20 countries qualify every four years to compete in four pools of five teams over a period of about two weeks. The Dominican Republic won in 2013, and the U.S. finished first in 2017. Both times Puerto Rico was the runner up, with Japan finishing third and the Netherlands fourth. Covid forced postponement of the 2021 event to 2023.

Pool play began March 7. Pool play is followed by a series of Round 2 contests, and two semifinals. The last two teams standing will compete in a single-game championship on March 21. Or so rumor has it. The format is so unusual by baseball standards that it makes one wonder if anyone really knows how it works. In fact, there is no consolation game to determine third and fourth place finishers. That's decided by committee. We all know how well that goes thanks to college football.

But, hey, it appears to be working. Ratings are on the rise along with interest among major league ballplayers in America. Games are broadcast by FOX Sports, so you know it's making money. Promoters are drooling over a possible Japan-US championship game, which would find Angels teammates and all-stars Mike Trout and Shohei Ohtani on opposing teams, with the former possibly batting against the latter!

In the meantime, the games can produce some interesting matchups, as well as total mismatches. For example, Great Britain (a rag tag team of dreamers, has-beens, wannabes, and a few prospects) is in the same pool with the U.S. (and its lineup of big-league all-stars whose only weakness may be pitching). There's a David vs. Goliath game at almost every turn, along with some interesting contests that fall into categories that can be intriguing for reasons both geographical and political. The pools are: Pool A – Chinese Taipei, Netherlands, Cuba, Italy, Panama; Pool B – Japan, Korea, Australia, China, Czech Republic; Pool C – USA, Mexico, Colombia, Canada, Great Britain; and Pool D – Puerto Rico, Venezuela, Dominican Republic, Israel, Nicaragua.

The biggest problem with the David vs. Goliath contests is that games are played with balls and bats, not slings and stones, and the goal is to outscore your opponents, not mortally vanquish them. There's little chance in many cases for victory by the underdog team, only some form of slight consolation. For example, Great Britain enjoyed a moment of encouragement on the first Saturday of play when they held the U.S. to six runs, and even took a lead for a time following a first-inning home run. But they lost 6-2 in a game that wasn't as close as the score would indicate. For some, however, it was seen as a sign of hope for a team representing a country in the early stages of developing a national baseball program.

The next day Great Britain went up against Canada (part of the British Commonwealth but in no mood to show any mercy to King or Motherland). After falling behind 3-0, Canada went on a scoring spree, taking a 16-8 lead into the fifth inning of a game that featured scoring in every half inning up till that point. Overall, it had more in common with a Super 60 softball matchup than high-level baseball, with a little Kraken on the side. Great Britain gave up 16 walks, as the game ended by mercy rule in the top of the seventh with Canada leading 18-8.

Regardless of the imbalance of team talent in the early going, that there even is a World Baseball Classic is further testimony of baseball's endearing qualities, enduring appeal, and general marketability. Billionaire owners don't allow their multi-millionaire stars to play out of a generosity of spirit. They allow them to participate with an eye for expanding markets and increasing profits. Based on crowd enthusiasm, especially in foreign lands, that's exactly what's happening.

For example, when Puerto Rico and Venezuela go at it just minutes after Canada disposes of Great Britain, raucous fans pack Marlins Park in Miami and hit decibel levels matched only by the most enthusiastic World Cup crowds. Fans in Japan, where television ratings for the event soar, are equally enthusiastic. So even when a game becomes a mismatch or a blowout, watching passionate fans go absolutely nuts can be attention-grabbing, until I'm ready to fall asleep. Then come the next day, I'll get up and play a version of this wonderful game that will get my day and, win or lose, another week of this winter journey off to an engaging start.

CHAPTER 13

Let's get it On

I wake up Monday morning feeling better physically than I have all year. There's no soreness from pulled leg muscles, including my (knock on wood) left hamstring. I consider not wrapping them at all. but decide to go with an ounce of prevention. Any decision to do otherwise would be frivolous and ill advised. Playing with younger men (I resist calling them kids) for one game doesn't turn back time. How young a person might feel between the ears has no bearing on anything going on from the neck down.

It is, however, wonderful not to feel sore or restricted. As I prepare for the game, I remind myself not to go all-out too abruptly, to ease through my physiological gears deliberately if not gradually. Do not, repeat, do not stomp the accelerator to the floor. Our 8:30 a.m. start, coupled with the spring-ahead weekend time change makes it feel even earlier. Moreover, when I get to the park, I learn I've misread the schedule and have arrived an hour early.

No matter. Have smart phone, can kill time anywhere. I check on the late Baseball Classic games and discover the big upset of the day is Mexico over Team USA, putting the dream Ohtani-Trout matchup in jeopardy and pressure on the American team to fulfill their on-paper potential.

I spend a little more time talking with players who actually do have an early start before some of my teammates begin arriving.

We head over to our field, help get it ready, and begin batting practice. Before long things are back to normal for our game against the Dodgers. The result will affect the standings only if the unlikely occurs: a Royals loss to the Orioles. Coupled with a victory by us, we would finish in first place, winning the regular season and the 2023 League Champions title and the jackets that come with it. Any other scenario and it all will come to the final game of the year against the Royals – winner takes all for the title because they own the head-to-head tiebreaker as a result of their earlier one-run victory the first time we met.

We have four losses this year and have beaten three of those teams in our second encounter. Beating the Royals in the final game would make it 4 for 4 in redemption games. But first we must deal with the Dodgers.

The game starts evenly as the Dodgers match the three runs we score in the top of the first with a three-spot of their own in the bottom half. Both teams play good defense and the game stays tight through the early innings, in which we take a 5-3 advantage. In the middle frames, both sides continue playing well in the field, but our hitters do a better job of making harder contact and finding more holes. We also do a better job of keeping balls we don't field cleanly in front of us and not giving away extra bases.

After several productive innings, we take a 14-5 lead into the top of the ninth. In the process, I realize that a change in my batting grip that seemed to feel really good had been causing my arms to disconnect from my body. I make a small adjustment and hit the ball extremely hard in my final two at-bats, the last one coming with two outs in the eighth and resulting in two RBI. We hold them scoreless in the bottom half of the inning, and then score six more times in the top of the ninth for a 20-5 lead that holds up for the final score.

The one big personal downside to the game comes when I re-pull my left hamstring in the eighth inning going first to third on a ball in the gap. I forget about going easy and try kicking it up a gear to score on the play. Instead, I come up lame 10 feet past second and limp my way slowly into third. When I get to the dugout I strap on another Ace bandage to give the area a bit more support and take to the field to finish the game.

My hamstring aside, the win continues a positive pattern of not only becoming healthier as a team, but better defensively. In the previous game we kept our opponent from scoring after the second inning. In this game, the Dodgers failed to score after the first inning. That's a lot of zeros for any form of baseball, and all the more unusual in what are generally high-scoring, slow-pitch softball contests. The big plays come from both the infield and outfield. Right fielder Gary Rocco, who was rendered almost immobile with foot problems early in the year, made an especially great play on a shot to right to end one inning.

Indeed, many of the guys made crisp, even impressive plays in the field. But the most crucial, and likely the most stellar, came from Sandy Hoad, who made a diving, rolling catch of a sinking line drive to center that appeared to be a sure hit. He's over 60, sure, but on this play had the sprawling, reckless form of a guy half his age.

The loss for the Dodgers drops their overall record to 10-7, good for the third seed in the league tournament next week. Based on winning the first half of the season, we're assured at least the second seed. Our overall record with one game remaining is 13-4. The Royals are one game back at 12-5. So the winner of the season's final game earns the regular season title and the championship jackets that come with it. The losers get the second seed and a tip of the imaginary hat.

In the parking lot where I'm unwrapping my legs after the game, Nick Layton strikes up a conversation while packing equipment into his car. He's a New Yorker and a diehard Yankees fan. He's also the league's assistant commissioner and is deeply involved in ensuring things go smoothly year after year. I believe his compensation for all his hard work is that, regardless of who drafts him, the team he lands on will be called the Yankees. I don't know it for certain, but some things you just know.

"Looks like it's you or the Royals for the season title," he says.

"Yeah, that would be nice," I reply. "But I keep telling myself that no matter what, this has been a great season, and we're just one team in a tiny league in a big, big world."

"That's true. I think a lot of the guys would say that," he replies, shutting the trunk and standing as tall as his 5-foot-3 frame will allow. "But every one of them, when they get out on the field, all they want to do is win."

"Yeah, you're right. I guess I'm just trying to keep things in perspective and stay loose," I say.

"Oh, I know I'm right. I see it all the time. I feel that way myself," he says, then breaks off into a brief soliloquy about how he already has the championship jackets, as well as the duffel bags that will go to the winning post-season tournament winner. He adds how sharp the jackets look and mentions the colors and a few other features. "You know. I can't remember if anyone has ever won both the regular season and the playoffs. I don't think they have." Then he says goodbye and climbs into his large, black, BMW sedan, leaving the last statement hanging like a challenge. But all I can think about as he drives away is that his 5-foot-3 frame somehow looks 6 feet tall when he's in the driver's seat of that car.

Tuesday comes around quickly enough, and a late-morning round of golf helps push the clock toward Wednesday and our rematch against the Royals. I play horrible golf, but that doesn't matter. I get to spend some time with Dallas Dodson, whom I met here in 2016. I enjoy his company because whether we agree on issues of the world or not, we respect each other's perspectives, listen to each other, and enjoy discussing just about any topic. On the golf course, he is an example of how to accept the moment for what it gives, be it a great shot and the satisfaction that goes with it, or a poor shot that offers the opportunity for a great recovery.

When the round is over we vow to play again soon. But given it took us two months to get this round on our calendars, I leave hoping for the best while knowing it could be a long time before we do it again.

I don't get back to my place until late afternoon. Following a quick shower, I cobble together a suitable dinner and decide to watch a bit of the World Baseball Classic, which at this point has me paying attention, but not fully engaged. It is, after all, an exhibition and I'm not the kind of fan who goes nuts chanting USA, USA, USA. I'm not a Russian spy, or radical terrorist, it's just that when it comes to sports, I'm more of a regionalist than a nationalist.

It's been that way since the 1980 Olympics. After the so-called Miracle on Ice, my passion began a steady decline likely connected to the influx of professionals into what had been truly amateur athletics, or at least a less-professional version. I realize that other countries were paying many of their athletes while operating national development programs and we were at a competitive disadvantage. I just got used to rooting for the USA as lovable, unpaid underdogs. I understand I'm in the minority now, but that's just how my internal flames of fandom burn.

When Wednesday morning finally arrives and I head out for our 8:30 game, the sun is still struggling to light up our little corner of southwest Florida. We're at the point in the calendar when the spring-ahead hour leaves us in the relative dark at 7 a.m. It's also chilly. But by the time we gather for batting practice, everyone is ready for our big game. A win gives us the regular season title and those jackets Nick thinks are at the apex of casual wear fashion, along with the added satisfaction of redemption wins over every team that has beaten us thus far. Of the four losses, the one to the Royals was the most irksome.

It was the one in which we compounded physical errors, which happen, with mental errors, which also happen from time to time, but in that game happened time after time after time. We were tied after nine innings and, in keeping with our pattern of the day, eventually lost due to base running and other mental lapses in the 9th and 10th. We were sloppy and they are just too good a team to play against that way. We remind ourselves of that going into this game. We also know that we're a better team than we were then.

Not only are we healthier, but we have consistently improved as a unit and, at this point in the season, have meshed our mix of eclectic personalities. We not only really enjoy playing and having fun together, but are also all about team – all of which is reflected in how we consistently root and encourage each other. We don't let anyone beat themselves up over a mistake, mental or physical – a graciousness made easier by a reduction in both kinds of errors. We constantly shout reminders of in-game situations, helping to maintain team focus. We aren't perfect by any means, but we're perfectly ready to pull together as a team and play as well as we're capable of on any particular day.

Both teams appear confident and ready as the game begins. We start out a bit shaky when Tommy's hurried throw from deep short sails wide of first. When he starts to beat himself up over it, I offer what encouragement I can, reminding him that there's nothing he can do about it now other than be ready to make the next play. The next batter hits a sinking line drive that cuts toward the right field foul line. Early in the year, the ball would likely get by the fielder and roll toward the fence with no one backing up the play. But that was then and this is now.

Gary Rocco, who started the season as lame as anyone, is now our right fielder. He charges in to attempt what looks to be an impossible play. But unlike earlier in the year, the right-center fielder is running to back him up. As Gary dives in the general direction of where the ball looks to be going, Bobby Voss charges toward the foul line. The best-case scenario appears to be that Bobby will get there and relay the ball back to the infield and keep any runs from scoring. But what happens is better than the best! As he heads to the ground, Gary sticks out his glove, snatches the ball in the webbing, rolls over, and gets to his feet, making an outstanding play that sets the tone for the game.

We hold them scoreless and put up two runs in the bottom half of the inning, keep it scoreless in the top of the second, and add another run in the bottom half for a 3-0 lead. It's a great early trend for us, but one that doesn't hold. Over the next six innings we manage only three more runs. Our bats don't go cold. It's more a case of they can play ball and make defensive plays, too. Neither team is perfect, but both play really well. As these games go, that would ordinarily lead to momentum shifts between teams. But this turns out to be no ordinary game.

The Royals mount scoring opportunities several times, but we always seem to make a solid or stellar play, both in the infield and outfield, to snuff out their threats. The upshot of it all is we find ourselves amassing an impressive collection of scoreless innings on defense. Eight in the previous game added to seven in the game before that, along with the eight complete in this game puts it at 23 out of 26 innings of shutout ball in our past three games! Just as they make plays to limit our scoring, we continue to make plays that hold them scoreless. We go to the top of the ninth with a shutout intact.

No one says a word. This is tantamount to a perfect game bid in the major leagues. Slow pitch softball is an offensive game. When one team holds another to six runs through eight innings, as they have held us, you expect to hold a lead. But time after time after time, we respond to threats big and small by making plays, as opposed to how we might have blown them early in the season. In the top of the ninth, the Royals seem primed to break the spell. With one out, they load the bases and are ready to send some of their better hitters to the plate. This is a game in which things can shift quickly, and the Royals appear prepared to do just that.

The next batter hits the ball hard to left field. Angelo Vitale, aching calves now at 90 percent, breaks in. From middle infield, I get a great perspective on balls in the air toward left. Over the course of the season, Angelo and I have worked out a pretty good system of communicating trajectory. If I shout "back, back, back," he trusts the call and breaks deeper in pursuit of the ball. If I shout "in" repeatedly, he continues to break in on the ball. On this play, I'm shouting "in, in, in," hoping he will keep the ball in front of him and limit the damage to a single run.

But this isn't Gimpy Angelo Version 101 out there. This is the 'I may be in my 60s, but I'm feeling kinda frisky' Angelo 202-Plus. As I continue to shout "in" he continues charging to attempt a play. One of two outcomes now appears likely: he keeps it in front of him (as he did on a similar play two games ago) and only one run scores, or it gets past him and three or four cross the plate.

There is, of course, a third and highly unlikely outcome. He could catch the ball, toss it into the infield, and prevent any runs at all from scoring. But the odds of that seem remote at best, almost as unlikely as shutting out a team as good as the Royals. But on this day, both things actually occur.

Angelo hurls his lanky, 6-foot-plus frame recklessly toward the ground, sticks out his glove an instant before impact, snatches the ball in his webbing, rolls over, and flips it to Tommy standing nearby. All runners scurry back to their bases in total disbelief. The next batter smashes a hard shot toward Tommy at short. He knocks it down, keeps it in front of him, and flips to me at second for the third out!

Final score: Phillies 6, Royals 0. The most unlikely of regular seasons comes to the unlikeliest of conclusions. In our final 27 innings of play, teams score against us in just three of those innings. The regular season is over. We earn our 2023 Naples Softball Championship jackets, and the seeds are set later in the day for an eight-team single elimination post-season tournament.

The next day I remain stunned by the shutout and how low scoring a game both teams played. I call Nick Layton to see if the league maintains season records that would confirm just how unusual our game had been. Verification isn't possible beyond the anecdotal. "This is my 11th year in the league. I don't recall anybody being shut out since I started playing in 2012," he says. "We're a pretty high-scoring league. Six runs as a winning total rings a bell. But I can't remember any shutouts."

Bobby Gentile, league secretary, is inactive now, but has a long history as a player. He too recalls some low-scoring games, but no shutouts. "It's the kind of thing you'd remember if it happened, I think. I know I'm not going to forget this one."

So here we stand, regular season champions and the No. 1 tournament seed. But we again have five days until our next game, a period that seems to take increasingly longer. Coincidentally, however, the World Baseball Classic has also finalized its field of eight. The four finalists on the Asian side of things are set to play ahead of teams from the West to help accommodate the winner's recovery from jet lag for the championship game scheduled in Miami. Japan continues to do its part to set up the Trout-Ohtani confrontation by beating Italy in its quarter final game. Trout and team USA are also in the quarter finals, but won't play Venezuela until Saturday, a game that conflicts with the Kraken's next start. What were the WBC schedule-makers thinking when they did that?

The choice of which to watch is easy. I choose the Kraken. I also choose the Kraken for a much-needed haircut, as I've gone unshorn since late December. I'm not bringing scissors to the game. I like these guys but have no plans for a group dugout cut. However, Peter and Dany Rivera, brothers who emigrated from Cuba with their mom and dad in 2001, are real-life barbers who operate a shop just south of the U.S. 41-Pine Ridge Road intersection in Naples.

Their common love of all things baseball is reflected in the name of their shop: Kaught Looking. The name pays homage to Jose Fernandez, a star pitcher with the Florida Marlins whose life and career ended abruptly following a tragic boating accident in 2016 when he was just 25 years old. The boat Fernandez owned and was piloting at the time of his death was called Kaught Looking.

In his final game on Sept. 20, Fernandez, also of Cuban heritage, worked eight shutout innings in a 1-0 game against the Washington Nationals, notching 12 strikeouts and giving up three hits and no walks. After the game he told a teammate it was the best outing of his career. The next morning, he was found dead. In the weeks after, a toxicology report obtained by ESPN revealed the presence of cocaine in his system along with alcohol levels twice the legal limit.

He finished 2016 with a major-league-best average of 12.49 strikeouts per nine innings, for a total of 253 Ks, while winning a career-best 16 games. His tragically short career line boasts a 38-17 record for a .691 winning percentage and a 2.58 ERA.

"He was the best," says Peter, the elder of the two at 33.

"We named the shop to honor him," says Dany, 27.

That was in December 2021. Just 15 months later, business continues growing and they're looking for barbers to staff some of the other chairs in the shop.

"We're at the point now where both our schedules are full most of the time," says Dany.

When I made an appointment online, my choices were Dany or "Other Staff." As I climb into his chair, both men share their immigration story. Their mother was a nurse in 2001 when she earned a visa to legally move to the United States, when Dany and Peter were 7 and 14, respectively.

"We didn't know anyone here," says Peter.

The process landed them in Naples, where Peter immediately looked for opportunities to play baseball. "I loved to play. I love the game," he says. He arrived here a Yankees fan because "that's the only team you hear about in Cuba. We had no internet, so everything was Yankees, Yankees, Yankees." But one of the first friends he made in the United States was a Red Sox fan who converted Peter, who in turn recruited his younger brother. When they hear I'm a Yankees fan, we laugh that I'm at the mercy of Dany's clippers, and I comment that I better not find a giant B etched into the back of my head.

As Dany continues cutting away, I look around the shop thinking how well assimilation works when newcomers to the U.S. have a functional system to assist them. They were happy to be placed in Naples. Other possibilities included Miami (a much larger city) or Kentucky, with a far different climate and culture than their home on the tiny Isla de la Juventud just to the south of the western end of the Cuban mainland. Their mother received assistance in finding not only a place to live, but also in securing work as a nurse.

Growing up, the young brothers spent the bulk of their time playing baseball whenever they could. It was, as the line goes in the film Field of Dreams, the one constant in their lives, along with their mother and father, of course. The brothers not only loved baseball, they played it very well. Now, in their spare time, they get to play it together. Maybe not at the same level as the Alou brothers did, but certainly with a kindred passion.

Neither brother has children. "We have a dog," says Peter. "Maybe someday."

"A dog is enough," chimes in Elizabeth, Peter's wife, who also works the shop's reception desk.

"He's getting married soon," says Peter of Dany. "So you never know."

From there the talk shifts to the Kraken and the team's Achilles' heel: the walk.

"I don't understand why they can't throw more strikes," Dany says of the team's pitching staff. "Too many curve balls," adds Peter.

It does seem to be the mystery of the season for their team. You

Dany (left) and Peter Rivera at their barber shop which they proudly named Kaught Looking in honor of Jose Fernandez, the late Florida Marlins pitching star who died in a 2016 boating accident at 25.

never know at what moment of the game the plate will seem to go missing, with none of their pitchers able to find it, until suddenly they do again. But somehow, no matter how many times they find it, they manage to lose it again. Both brothers can add no clues.

"Maybe they'll find it tonight," I say in reference to their 6 p.m. game.

"No. It's been canceled," says Peter. "We don't have enough players."

I'm surprised, to say the least. I knew Dany pulled a hamstring in their last game and would be out. I also knew that Bruce Ingleright had a tournament with a different team on the other side of the state. However, Brandon Coraluzzo, their best pitcher, is also unavailable. Then Peter confesses that he and Dany are going to the WBC game that night in Miami for the USA-Venezuela contest. They also have tickets for the game between Cuba and the winner of Saturday's game on Sunday.

"Who are you rooting for?" I ask.

"Tonight the USA; tomorrow Cuba," says Peter. Dany quickly agrees.

They're not too surprised when I tell them I'll also be rooting for Cuba on Sunday and Venezuela on Saturday, fully grasping the concept of going with the underdog. But to my surprise, when I explain how I acquired my affinity for favoring the underdog over country of origin, they know all about the Miracle on Ice.

"From the movies," says Peter.

The haircut is a good one, excellent in fact; and reasonably priced by Naples' standards. On my way out we enjoy a few more laughs, say our goodbyes, and I offer my well-wishes for safe travels and a great time at the games in Miami. I drive away thinking that the Rivera brothers are, as my friend Denny likes to put it, "living the dream."

I also head out better informed about possible gaps in the Kraken's schedule and their potential effects on the rest of my weekend plans. Their Saturday game is definitely canceled. Sunday is still a go for an afternoon makeup game. Looking over their schedule, they could have as few as two games left: the makeup and the wild-card playoff game on March 26. I decide to attend both.

As difficult as it feels to believe, March is creeping by and soon will be over, which means so too will our softball season and my time in Florida. But there's no arguing about the schedule or the calendar. I could have as many as three playoff games remaining, or as few as one if we lose the first single-elimination game. So with the shadows of inevitability hanging over the coming days, off I go to the Kraken's Sunday afternooner.

They're once again short-handed with only seven players. Two of them are stand-ins, players being recruited by Joe to join the team next season. They ask me if I want to play. I again say I will if the opposing team agrees. This time their opposition insists on the forfeit, agreeing to play the game for practice, but only if two of their players can join the Kraken lineup. I'm out; they're in. It's maybe a little disappointing, but I'm also a bit relieved not to be risking injury with a game of my own scheduled for early the next day.

The Kraken open with Christian Cotto taking the mound. I've given him the nickname Mr. Cot-tio, with the emphasis on the final syllables as in Mr. Kot-tee-air in the old television show "Welcome Back Kotter." Some of the players are familiar with the reference, thanks to the world of never-ending reruns. It appears to be sticking.

He gets through the first three outs with no walks, which I believe is a first. If not, it's the first time in a long time. But once again the strike zone tightens and the plate gets lost. With so many players absent, team spirit also seems lacking. They do their best to cheer each other on, but their efforts seem just a bit fabricated, further weakened by the opposition's offense and offering up of two players.

They manage to battle back a bit and score a few runs. In the end, despite another loss, the Kraken remain hopeful that they can reorganize and make a solid showing in the playoffs. Perhaps also, the shift in the calendar from winter to spring will give them a lift. You know what they say about hope springs eternal. My own focus shifts to our first playoff game scheduled for 9:30 a.m. Monday, March 20, which actually does mark the first day of spring.

When I get back to my apartment there's an email from my friend Bob with a story from the San Francisco Chronicle attached. The headline reads: You Get Attached: How Giant's Brandon Crawford Builds Trust in his Glove. Bob is the same friend I mentioned early on who still has his Wilson A2001 glove from Little League and high school displayed prominently on a bookshelf in his home. As I begin reading I think maybe there's something in the Bay Area air that affects such attachments. After all, it was there that Mike Gallego risked life and limb to retrieve his glove during an earthquake.

Crawford also takes his relationship with his glove seriously but doesn't match Gallego's devotion. The article puts it this way:

While Crawford's glove means a lot to him, he's not so romantic about it that he gives it a nickname, talks to it or sleeps with it, as other players over the years have been known to do.

"I've never really done that, but I definitely want to protect it as much as I can," Crawford said. "When I pack for a road trip, I'll typically put a baseball in the pocket and stuff socks around it so it's not folded the wrong way when we get to the next city. It's not like I put it in my backpack and take it aboard the plane with me. Or sleep with it."

I read the article and proudly take my place among those players who name their gloves. I'm with Crawford with regard to not sleeping with it and, as I said earlier, my verbal interactions fall well short of conversation. I've also decided that when I return home, Bader will occupy a warm place in the main living area, no longer banished to basement life among old golf clubs and other extraneous possessions destined for a trip one day to Goodwill or some other second-hand store.

However, with the report of another injury to Harrison Bader, I'm beginning to question my naming decision.

Eventually I make dinner and pass the evening with the USA-Cuba WBC game playing in the background. The game is close early, but the Americans clearly have the stronger team, and on this night, the favorites win the game, moving things closer to the much-desired Ohtani-Trout confrontation.

I confirm the start time for our game against the Tigers the next day and set an alarm before heading to bed with my own hope springs eternal dancing in my head for a good night's sleep on this last official night of winter.

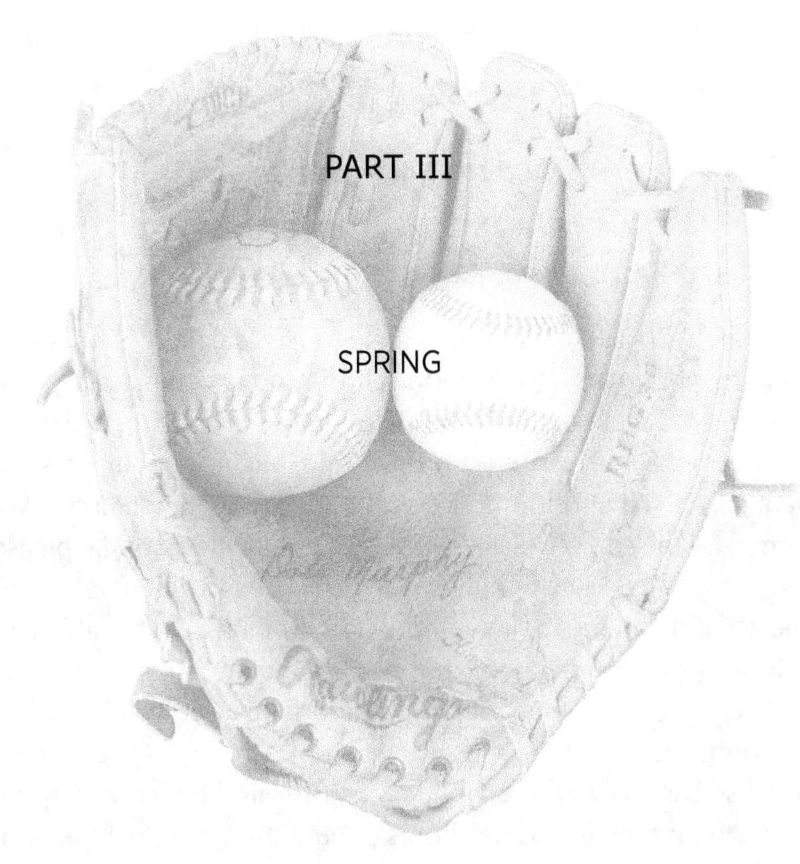

PART III

SPRING

CHAPTER 14

And the Beat goes On

It's March 20 and a lot's happening. The calendar says spring has arrived. Friends back north tell me to cease being silly, that I should stop taunting them because I know that spring will never really come to the western shores of Lake Michigan. Oh, buds will eventually swell and turn to flowers and leaves, temperatures will warm, and the seasons will change. But not anytime soon – please, stop the teasing. They're right of, course. Spring will arrive around June 19 and Summer will get there around June 22. I say this with a bit of tongue in my cheek, but not too much. Waiting for spring in Wisconsin, and a lot of other northern states, can be like waiting for Godot.

I also say this in the belief that, apart from how cruel a spring my northern friends and neighbors endure, they also feel the hope that finds our hearts in springtime regardless of the weather. No matter how cold or damp our April and May remain, the promise of new growth and new life makes it possible to find a silver lining in every cloud, real or metaphorical.

Meanwhile, here in southwest Florida, there's a feeling of a more northern spring in the air. The temperature as I head out to our first playoff game is in the lower 50s, a heat wave by northern standards, but car heater weather down here. I arrive early to circulate a Sharpie and the game ball I heisted following our season clincher against the Royals for everyone to sign and present to Howard Goldstone, our manager.

This heist was no easy task. The game's head umpire was doggedly diligent in his attempt to retrieve both balls (as is his near-sworn duty). Meanwhile, I was trying to abscond with the one from the final out, a toss to me at second base. He kept searching amid our celebration, but eventually gave up. Five days later, everyone signed it and, following batting practice, Howard received his memento just before we took the field for single-elimination tournament game No. 1. Win and we keep going. Lose and we exit early.

From the start, something feels off. It's hard to identify. We aren't in a total funk, not even a daze. It's more of a slight hangover. We don't quite get to balls we might have reached with just a slightly better jump or first step. What should be a routine throw from third to first flies inexplicably five feet over the first baseman. Just like that, the Tigers put the maximum five runs on the board, and we're in a big hole.

We come back with three in the bottom of the first, but it feels like it should have been more. We just aren't clicking in ways we ordinarily do. We've gone from sleek sports car on a fast track to backfiring Model T on a muddy, turn-of-the-century dirt road. The nice thing about Model Ts, though, is that they were a simple car. Even when broken down, they could usually be repaired on the spot with a few simple tools that came with the car – that essentially is our challenge.

So, after backfiring our way through the early innings, we clean off the spark plugs, kick some mud off our tires, tighten a few bolts, and soon get rolling on our way. By the fifth inning we're maintaining a slight lead and even begin building on it a little. We take a five-run advantage into the top of the ninth and withstand a mild threat before wrapping things up with an 18-14 win. It ends on the first ball hit to me all game that I could make a play on – a ground ball just to the right side of second base – a true ground ball that keeps rolling and hopping its way over an infield known for bad hops and misdirection.

When I field it and turn to flip to Tommy covering second, his eyes are bulging and there's a strange look of anxiety on his face, even though the runner's still a good two and a half steps from the base when the ball gets to him.

"Jeez!" he shouts after the out, with a combination of joy and relief. "I didn't think that thing was ever going to get to you!"

"It was going to get there," I assure him. "But it wasn't going to get through me when it did." Indeed, I had stayed down on the ball, crouched low, glove nestled on the dirt between my legs, patiently waiting to make a play, my deliberateness being the source of most of Tommy's angst. But I knew the batter was slower than the runner on base, and if the out at second wasn't an option when the ball got to me, the play at first would be.

In the end, we get our spring off to a good start. We work through our sluggishness and manage the first of what we now hope will be our final three wins of the season, and a tournament victory to go with our 2023 season championship. Meanwhile, we aren't the only team stuck in a little mud this day.

The Royals are mired in a battle with the Yankees, the No. 7 seed, but a dangerous team despite their overall sub-.500 record. In fact, the Royals first-half inning mirrors ours, as they go down by five runs before getting to bat. However, they fail to score in their half of the first and their second at-bat as well, extending their scoreless inning streak after their season finale against us to 11. They were trailing 8-0 when they finally scored in their half of the third to make it 8-3. They outscored the Yankees the rest of the way, but couldn't overcome the early deficit, ultimately ending up on the short end of a 14-10 game.

That outcome, combined with our win, means the Yanks will

be our second-round opponent, and a potentially difficult one at that. On the surface they look like a Jekyll and Hyde team. Good enough to win two out of three against the Royals, including their playoff win, yet erratic to the point of finishing the year with the third-worst record in the league.

The truth is, their story isn't one about split personalities so much as vanishing ones. Be it family obligations, injury, business demands, or illness, throughout the year, some of their best players would go MIA at different times, with as many as four gone at the same time. Even now, as our game approaches, there's a concern that they will be down their leadoff batter/left fielder, who will be in Pittsburgh on business. The other game matches the Dodgers, who disposed of the Red Sox 24-12 in the first round, against the Cubs, who won their game against the Orioles 20-19.

In between all this was the final game of the WBC. Being a regionalist, I wasn't emotionally invested in a win by the USA. The final score of 3-2, by Japan over Team USA was, in my mind, a matter of someone had to win. There could be no surprise had the game gone the other way. I couldn't help but think, however, that the Japanese beat the rest of the world because they play baseball in a way more reminiscent of what talking heads call "old school." Of course, that's an opinion of an "old guy" who enjoyed watching Japan's emphasis on contact at the plate and dedication to doing all the little things on both offense and defense that can make the difference between winning and losing.

As for the big matchup between Shohei Ohtani and Mike Trout, drama junkies got their moment of high theater with a two-out, ninth inning, swinging strikeout of Trout to end the game. It became a much-talked-about moment. But in fairness to Trout, it was among the more likely outcomes in such a scenario – dramatic, but likely. It doesn't require sabermetrics, just the basic acknowledgment that failure at bat is far more likely than success, especially when measured against the probability of a game-tying home run. It was, however, great in-the-moment stuff for Japan and Ohtani, whose team earned and occupied center stage in the sports world and deservedly so, in a come-full-circle moment.

America brought the game to Japan in the 1870s and gave it another big boost in 1934 when Babe Ruth led a team of all-stars on an exhibition tour there. All the Japanese have done since is embrace the game, fall in love with it, and play it the right way. Yes, that's a vague term, for sure. But watch a few games played by Japanese teams, even at the Little League level, and you'll see clear examples of what it means to play the game the right way.

Moreover, the tournament itself demonstrated that, as far as global enthusiasm goes, baseball holds its own against all comers. These global competitions are not going to go away just because a few players get injured. Players get injured all the time, even in spring training. Fans are beginning to want this thing, not just in Japan (where it has been embraced from the start), or Latin America (where wildly enthusiastic rooting interests of smaller countries almost defy imagination), but in the U.S. as well.

Here in America, a "dream team" got beat. For whatever reason, Americans don't generally distinguish very well between losing at sport and losing in other, more meaningful facets of life. We often equate things that matter in the vast scheme of things with things that don't. Maybe it's all those years of national anthems before games. Maybe it's the flyovers before the start of major sporting events, or honoring heroes during the seventh inning stretch or halftime breaks, or some combination of these and other traditions. Whatever might cause it, there's no telling when our national psyche can be triggered and something that didn't matter just yesterday suddenly becomes a priority.

It happened with basketball when college kids from the U.S. were outmatched by players from other countries who were essentially professionals playing in the Olympics. Next thing you know, there was Michael Jordan and the Dream Team. It happened with both men and women's soccer. And it is about to happen with baseball. This year's U.S. lineup was a pitcher's nightmare, with all-stars from top to bottom. But American pitchers of the highest caliber stayed with their teams in spring training, not wanting to risk injury or interruptions in their training programs.

There's no way, given the attention the event earned in 2023, that the U.S. teams in the future will not have some of the country's best pitchers playing alongside their best position players. Maybe teams will be forced into early spring training or make some other change in their training regimens. But when the Classic is played next in 2026, place a futures bet now if some sports book will introduce the line, that at least half of all American pitchers, both starters and relievers, will rank among the top 10 in their field.

Enough of the Classic for the present, though. Yesterday's dead and gone; tomorrow's out of sight, and, today, albeit with slightly more local enthusiasm, the four finalists in the Collier County Super Senior Softball Classic (OK I made that name up) are ready to play ball in round two of their single-elimination tournament. Fan attention will be riveted, at least for a very few, on the outcomes of today's games between the Phillies and Yanks on one field of beautiful North Collier Regional Park, and the Dodgers and Cubs on another just to our south.

We start with a simple goal: win every inning. We also start without Angelo in left field. He reinjured his calve muscles in the first tournament game and is not able to take the field in this one.

The Yankees come out strong, score a run quickly and mount a threat. But two good plays on well-hit balls limit the damage to just one run. We score three in our half of the first and win inning No. 1. They score two more in the top of the second and we go to our half of the inning tied. We counter with the maximum five runs in our turn at bat, but it feels less like an eruption than a bit of self-destruction on their part with some very unusual errors on seemingly simple plays. A dropped toss at second base and a mishandled fly ball by a generally sure-handed outfielder, coupled with some big hits to capitalize on the errors, all aid our cause.

We hold them scoreless in the next two innings, putting up two runs in each of our at-bats for what begins to feel like a comfortable 12-3 lead after four. But they get their mojo back in the top of the fifth with four runs and cut the deficit to 12-7. Then they hold us scoreless in the bottom half, winning the inning and bringing the game back within reach.

Neither team scores in the sixth, keeping things tight. It gets tighter still when they put up two more runs in the top of the seventh. With the score 12-9, we again feel a sense of urgency. They've not only made it a close game; they've also turned their order over and will be sending their better hitters to the plate in the eighth.

It becomes a game of punch-counterpunch. We come back with three runs and, just as expected, their top-of-the-order produces with three more in the top of the eighth. Then it's counterpunch time again, as once more we respond with three runs.

We take the field in the ninth with a comfortable, though not insurmountable lead. All they need is a hit here and there and things could get uncomfortable in a hurry. Even though they score two more runs, we make some plays and hold off their threat for an 18-14 win that feels a lot closer than the score.

The web-gem of the game happens on one of their final three outs, with Jim "I have 7 kids, 20 grandkids, and 22 great grandchildren" Neuser behind the plate. Jim has made maybe two clean catches all season, depending on how clean is defined – one on a pop-up about eight feet in the air; the other on a foul tip with two strikes he juggled a bit and then hung onto. Usually on pops ups, Jim will look to the sky, hold out his glove, and teeter about arms extended and waving, resembling some ancient mariner on shore leave after too much rum. When we come off the field, he'll say something like, "Did you see me on that foul ball? I was like a cat." Then with suitable if not perfect timing, add, "But I gotta learn to lay off of that catnip."

Jim's final web gem of the season comes not on a pop up or foul tip, but on a bullet of a one-hop throw from Tommy on a relay from the outfield. Often on such plays, Dave Smith, our pitcher, will rush to cover home. Not on this one. With the ball flying in Jim's direction, there is no Dave to be seen. The throw is coming so fast that my first thought is of fear for Jim's safety. But Jim plants his foot on the base, bends, and somehow makes a clean, short-hop scoop of the ball. He looks at his glove and maybe the expression on his own face is one of greater surprise than on anyone else's. The rest of us, I believe, are too astonished to immediately react at all. Moreover, Jim is so stunned when the out call is made that he's temporarily speechless for the first time all season.

Of course that doesn't last very long. Just a few moments later he's prattling on about how he had it all the way. In the end, we wound up with a hard-fought victory which, coupled with a 17-9 Dodgers win over the Cubs, sets up a final game on March 27 between the first- and third-place regular season finishers.

Where are you, ESPN and FOX Sports?

They're nowhere to be found. But come Monday, the day of the final tournament game, WINK, the local CBS affiliate has promised they will be. They're not so much interested in the game as they are in doing a brief feature on one of our players: none other than Jim "Noisier-Than-Most" Neuser. Apparently someone has shared with them via their story suggestion line, that Jim is newsworthy for all his non-athletic, outside-the-lines charm and contributions. I know who that someone is, but I'm not saying.

However, that's still several days away and, as usual, there's a Kraken game on Sunday to help pass some of the time. It's their wild card playoff game against the Braves. The Kraken are the bottom seed but show up with a lot of enthusiasm despite being down several of their better players. Dany Rivera's hamstring won't be healed till next season. Additionally, Bruce Ingleright broke a rib playing in a tournament the previous weekend and is also done for the year. On top of that, Brandon Coraluzzo, perhaps their best pitcher, is also unavailable.

The situation presses Max Troiano into an emergency start. He goes to the mound in the bottom of the first with a 2-0 lead. The diminutive force of nature is a little on edge to begin, but eventually settles into a nice rhythm, helping the Kraken maintain an early lead. He's also amped up for some high-speed antics on the base paths, resulting in a uniform that's covered with far more than his usual amount of dirt.

Overall, the game unfolds in a way that breaks with the Kraken's form of combining too many walks with untimely mental and physical errors. The result is something they're not used to: holding a lead. In fact, they hang onto it early on before falling behind 3-2 after three innings and 5-2 after five.

But good things happen when you're playing loose and getting walks rather than surrendering them. The Kraken are happily putting pressure on the opposing defense rather than feeling it themselves. Things can get better still when you play smart, alert defense. The breakout performance of the day in the field comes from Phil Viar, a bulky first baseman who has the unusual habit of wearing a button-down collar, long-sleeve sports shirt under his uniform jersey (a look he somehow pulls off). He makes several scoops of throws in the dirt to prevent outs from becoming throwing errors. But his gem of the day is somehow recording an out at first base on an unassisted putout, then baiting a runner on third to get lost in a rundown and become a rally-killing third out.

The Kraken eventually tie the score with a three-run seventh. Even Christian Cotto, who took over pitching duties in the sixth, possesses far more control than usual to limit his walks. Then he does the totally unexpected at the plate. With two on and two out in the top of the eighth, he launches a 3-2 pitch over the left field wall for a three-run homer and an 8-5 lead. The jubilation is explosive and equally fun to watch.

My plans are to return north at the end of the upcoming week. I joke with them that I might have to extend my stay for their playoff run. I even think that I might. This is a team that has stuck together and kept the faith despite a string of disheartening losses. They adopted me as a player for a game and an unofficial bench coach after that. They've laughed, joked with each other, and kept one another's spirits from tumbling through several rough stretches. Finally, it looks like it's their time to transform faith in their talents into an outcome that demonstrates their faith is well-founded.

Then it starts to slip away. The Braves load the bases on walks in the bottom of the ninth, as Christian Cotto once more can't find the strike zone. Unlike past fits of wildness, however, many of the balls seem close to being strikes and his control isn't totally gone – just off enough that he attempts to force-find the plate to prevent walking in a run. It's not even a really bad pitch under the circumstances, just a necessary one that catches enough of the plate and bat to yield a high fly to relatively deep left.

Nate Cox drifts back to catch it, drifts some more, and then a little more. But a brisk, hot spring Florida wind keeps carrying the ball beyond his reach and over the fence, blowing away the Kraken's joy of a few outs ago to their opponent's side of the field, as only a game-winning, walk-off grand slam can do.

To their credit, almost everyone on the team hangs around and talks about what could have been. Not wanting to leave, they instead gather for a team picture and dawdle a bit in packing up their equipment. But other teams are waiting to use the field. So just like that, and just like his grandfather's Brooklyn Dodgers of the 1950s, Joe Pignatano and his 2023 Southwest Florida Kraken must set aside their dreams and wait till next year.

Just maybe, 2024 will be their 1956. Hey, you never know. As another one of his grandfather's teams bellowed repeatedly in 1969, "You gotta believe!"

Meanwhile, it begins to hit me that win or lose, in less than 24 hours my own season will also be over. With Major League Baseball's Opening Day less than a week away, there will be plenty of baseball to watch and be entertained by. But the preparation and playing days that have been so much a part of my life these past five or so months will be over. I do my best to set these thoughts aside.

There's one more game to play, a present to stay in, and another day of purpose for Bader and his leathery life.

CHAPTER 15

Action, Camera, Play Ball!

The television news reporter shows up as promised and Jim delivers as only he can. What one might think would be a quick in-and-out interview continues through most of the pre-game warm-ups and batting practice hour. From a distance, it's hard to tell if the reporter can't get Jim to stop talking or if he keeps asking questions because he's fallen under Jim's oratorical spell. Either way, it's a symbiotic relationship – the results of which we'll all get to see in the hours following the game.

But now it's time to play ball.

From the first pitch, it's obvious that things are going to go the way of the unexpected. But that is how any form of this game works. You can choose your AI program, plug in all the data, predict an outcome, and get it right every time – until you don't. Moreover, the forces that produce baseball's unpredictable and unexpected moments are as mysterious as the outcomes they affect. Additionally, those forces will always recur anytime, anywhere, in innumerable forms with no dependable rhythm or cycle, for as long as the game is played.

We have Angelo back in left field and Noah in center, promising to solidify what had, in our previous game, been an effective but patchwork outfield. Then just as if it had been scripted, the Dodgers leadoff batter lofts a fairly well hit line drive to left. Angelo makes a perfect read, breaks in on the ball with a measured gait, and raises his glove for the catch. When his legs are right, it's fun to watch the energy and grace he demonstrates in the field. This day he felt his ailing calf muscles had healed enough to give it a go, and with the first batter, that looks to be the case. Mitt raised to perfectly intersect with the path and arc of the descending sphere, the first out looks to be in the books.

Then it all begins to go off script. Just as Angelo's about to make the catch, his right leg buckles, his glove drops about an inch, and the ball deflects off the webbing. Angelo crumbles to the ground, writhing in pain and grasping his leg. The runner winds up on third base. Angelo needs assistance just to make it to the dugout bench, where he will sit for the rest of the game, icing his leg, and cheering us on.

The inning continues with more of the unexpected. We walk two batters. Dave, our pitcher, rarely issues walks. Next, a ball Tommy would expect to almost always get to eludes his glove and trickles past him. A couple of balls we might have caught on other days for outs drop in for hits. They score three runs. We match their output in our half of the inning and take the field in the second thinking perhaps we've righted the ship.

We hold them to one run in the second, but it's a struggle; then we fail to score in our turn at bat. Back in the field for the third, we combine walks with horrible fielding and they put up four runs, which we again match in our half of the frame. A third of the way through a game that feels more like a slog through a humid, bug-infested jungle than a walk in the park, we've played our worst, had most bounces go against us, but trail by only a single run.

After four innings, the margin is two, and things look like they're about to get worse, as we kick the ball around a bit in the top of the fifth. They load the bases with one out. Their next batter fouls off two successive pitches with two strikes, by rule a strikeout in our league. One more out and we're out of the inning. Next up is a hard-hitting lefty who rips a bullet down the right field line. Ordinarily, our right fielder would be Gary Rocco, who on two good legs with his usually strong arm might be expected to hustle to the line, field it cleanly as it rolls through the outfield, and return it to the infield, maybe limiting the damage to a single run.

But Gary's also nursing two bad legs and is playing first base for the second straight game. The rocket down the line never gets past him. He dives, rolls over in a cloud of red infield dust, and makes the most spectacular fielding play any of us has seen all year. We rush to the dugout with the entire team converging along the way to shower him in a wave of approving screams, high fives, and fist bumps. No doubt, if we weren't so collectively lame as a team, a couple of jumping hip-bumps might have also made the scene.

The play emotionally rejuvenates and convinces us that this is the catalyst that will launch us to victory. After all, they're the same team we held to eight consecutive scoreless innings near the close of the season. Instead, we do something we haven't done all year – fail to score in four successive innings. Even the infusion of adrenaline from Gary's absolutely remarkable play couldn't get our offense going. We also resume our struggles on defense. The Dodgers score in each of the next three innings and take a seven-run lead. We come to bat in the bottom of the eighth down seven runs.

Then, true to our season-long form, we make a final run at a comeback. We're already the season champions. We've earned the title jackets that are this league's equivalent of Championship Rings. In doing so, we won first-half season honors, second-half season honors, and the overall season championship. We may not be the 1927 Yankees, but by Collier County Super 60 Softball standards, we're pretty darn close! The sundae is ours. A tournament victory would be the cherry on top. We come to bat in our half of the eighth ready to give it our best shot.

As it turns out, our best shot is pretty darn good. We hit, we cheer, we score; we hit, score, and cheer some more en route to a breakout, high-production inning. Despite the walks, despite all the bad bounces, pulled muscles, scoreless innings, and various other mishaps, we've made it a one-run game. Going to the last inning, the Dodgers' lead is 15-14.

But in the end, that's as close as we get. The final inning is a microcosm of the worst parts of the first seven and a half. Whether they hit the ball hard or soft, none of the bounces goes our way. Everything that might fall for a hit finds grass. What could have been a quick, scoreless top of the ninth, becomes a bad-bounce, elusive ground ball, dink and dinger fest for the Dodgers that results in a lot of runs for them, followed by a round of scoreless futility for us.

After the game, we say our good-byes as a team, but many of us decide to go to a local sports pub for lunch and a more leisurely farewell. Jim Neuser joins us and is in the clouds about his interview and scheduled appearance on the local news that evening. We spend some time licking our wounds and tossing around a few what-ifs, but soon make the present not about the day, but the season. None of us wants any of it to end. Someone reminds us that pick-up games resume Wednesday morning, but playing alongside anyone else but each other fails to register as an appealing idea. A few minutes later, the check comes, we do the math, and we're off to the parking lot going our separate ways.

Later that afternoon, I turn on the television and execute a successful search for the news feature on Jim. And there he is in all his verbal glory. There's footage of Jim cracking jokes in the dugout; footage of him insisting the ump penalize an opposing player five yards for delay of game.

The reporter informs viewers that Jim has been playing senior softball for 35 years and continues to do so at 89. When he asks Jim why, he responds, "For love of the game. And of course, the players.

You don't get this kind of camaraderie at a bar or someplace. You know, this is where you're going to do-or-die for the team."

The reporter informs the audience of Jim's affection for talking trash in a way that he somehow pulls off as more charm than harm. "I'm not a quiet ballplayer," admits Jim. And just like that he transitions from hyperbole to understatement.

A soundbite from a fellow league member adds that hitting when Jim's catching involves a constant stream of jabber. "Every time you get up, he tries to tell you jokes. He tries to distract you from hitting the ball. That's his thing." One form of it, anyway.

He completes his interview saying, "This has added 10 quality years to my life at least." The reporter closes by telling viewers Jim thinks he has at least another year in him.

I'm guessing he has more. And when it's finally over for him, on and off the field, he'll do his own spin on the line about the old ballplayer telling his teammates that if they want him to stop playing, they'll have to tear the uniform off his back. I see it going down this way.

Jim will simply play until he can't stand up or he develops lockjaw. In the end, he'll insist on being buried in his Phillies jersey. There'll be a big wake, with an open coffin, and a lot of storytelling, tears and laughter. After everyone leaves, the undertaker at the crematorium shuts the coffin and wheels it to the fiery mouth of the open furnace. Jim will have pre-arranged a way to have the lid flip open, his body sit up, and a recording of his voice cry out, "Fire? You call this a fire? Let me tell you how to make a fire!"

And out he'll go in a blaze of glory.

CHAPTER 16

There's got to be a Morning After

Tuesday feels different this week. For the first time in months, there's no game tomorrow. Nor will the Kraken play this Sunday. I'm not a beach person beyond walking. I don't own a boat. Golf courses haven't cut their rates yet and remain overbooked, overpriced, and now, in some cases, beaten up from excessive play. The ebb and flow of daily life to which I've grown familiar has suddenly developed too much ebb and too little flow.

I have no demands on my time or plans for replacement activities in what has been my weekly routine. Having already visited old haunts and connected with a few friends, there's not a lot of unfinished personal business left to handle either. More and more, it's feeling like the time to return north is nearing.

Last week, the league issued a reminder that Wednesday begins a return to informal pick-up games for any players who just want to show up, choose sides, and continue to play some softball. A typical league season kicks off with similar informal contests every November when the weather cools and seasonal residents begin returning. Players get a chance to round themselves into shape. I'm pretty sure those who participate in these games prior to the annual player draft and team assignments are less prone to the kind of injuries our team constantly faced.

But I've already decided not to participate in this round of post-season pick-up play. Monday's game has left me with another slight muscle pull and scant enthusiasm for playing ball – a feeling that has carried over into Tuesday like one of those headache-less hangovers the morning after a night of overeating and a tad too much wine. You know, those mornings where you wander around in a bit of a funk a half-step behind the rest of the reawakening world. I simply couldn't deny my sudden lack of interest in playing softball. My journey had specific goals around playing, all of which had been met.

Later Tuesday morning, I wash my jersey, collect all my equipment and bandages in my canvas game-day bag, and stuff it all deep into my car trunk behind my golf clubs, a collapsible camping chair, and several bags of other items I won't need until well after I've returned home. I continue through the day dividing my attention between enjoying the warm weather and doing little things to prepare for the long drive north. Then somewhere around mid afternoon a voice from within begins to make itself heard and express a different point of view.

It admonishes me for my assessment of pickup games as somehow unworthy of my time. I slowly begin believing if anything, they're imminently worthy. I'm reminded of something Jim said in his interview about how playing in this league makes him feel "like I'm playing in high school yet." If that's so, I begin telling myself, then post-season, informal pickup games might take us back farther yet to times of our most youthful innocence.

I go to my car, open the trunk, push aside my golf clubs and camping chair, move a couple of random items, and retrieve my game bag.

The next day I awake, dress, grab my gear, and head out for the ball fields, where I'm one of the first half dozen or so players to arrive. Some are already setting up the field. For a while it looks like there won't be enough people to field two teams. But shortly, others begin arriving at a slow, steady rate – some in their team jerseys, others in comfortable, non-affiliated tee shirts. Everything moves to a gentler rhythm than in the regular season.

Noah is there. Monday he beat himself up after the game for a misplayed ball in the final blowout inning, as if his single misplay created our unholy mess. Now he's back in his usual good spirits, everything in perspective, happy to be here. We chat some about the year and what fun it has been. It's good to see him smiling again. Bob Voss is there as well, but his wife, Sharon, is off helping to care for family in Missouri. By the time she returns, I'll be gone. I tell him to give her my best and that I hope to see them both again next year.

When we finally divide into teams, there's no sense of urgency or mindset of "us against them." This is a good thing because Noah and Bob are on the other team and I wouldn't want to see them as the opposition in any sense of the word. Another difference in this new world of pickup play, the first team bats for two half innings. Then the team in the field comes in and does the same. Two sets of three outs per side. Who says old people are set in their ways?

Just as I suspected it would be, the atmosphere is one less reminiscent of organized play and more akin to those long ago times when we would knock on neighborhood doors, recruit players, fan out in larger numbers, knock on more doors, and eventually gather on our makeshift ballfield adjacent to the creek that ran through our side of town.

There was little consistency to such efforts in terms of how many players might assemble on any given day. Seven per side and we had rules that allowed us to play the whole field; fewer and we made adjustments. With four per side, batters had to choose which side of second base they would hit to. If they failed to put the ball in play on their side of choice, it was an out regardless of how hard or far the ball went. Even if there were only two of us, so long as we had a ball, bat, and glove, we'd figure something to do that was derivative of the game.

My childhood reminiscences fade and my thoughts return to where I stand, basking in the sunshine and the surrounding landscape of the park. There's an egret in the distance, an osprey returning to a nest atop one of the light towers on a remote soccer field, and a fresh breeze in the air. As I continue soaking in the sights and sounds around me, it becomes clear that this is my goodbye to everything that has been these past several months.

These players, and maybe several others who couldn't make it today, will continue to gather here on Mondays and Wednesdays. They'll continue to play, just as they did as kids, some variation of this wonderful game of baseball. They'll joke around, even get childish at times, because that's much of the reason why they're here. They'll play together until the heat of spring turning toward summer is too great and their numbers too few, and many of the remaining seasonal residents head to their northern homes.

The joy of the moment fills me. The confluence of nature and the most amazing game in the world is indeed a gift to behold. But I also accept that my time in this several-month-long journey is rapidly coming to an end.

I play, I laugh, I say my goodbyes. And I leave the field, knowing that what began months ago with the simple act of rubbing oil into an old baseball glove is winding to a close. The next time I pack my game bag and set it deep in the trunk of my car, it will stay there until I've returned home. There will be no more drives to the ballfield on Monday and Wednesday mornings, only the long drive north. It's definitely time to head home, where there'll be no teammates to high five, only my cat Vanzetti, whom I hope misses me as much as I'll miss all this.

EPILOGUE

Wait Till Next Year

I began my trip home on March 31, the day after the start of the new major league baseball season. Opening Day is special. It's all about celebration and hope – kind of like the clock striking midnight on New Year's but without the miserable hangover, or the rapid reminder that things really haven't changed. A couple of days into any calendar New Year and the news makes it clear that the metaphorical leaf we just turned over isn't a new one, but the other side of the same one.

Opening Day is different, a better brand of New Year. Stadium parking lots are crowded with tailgaters and partiers. In the stands, capacity crowds are primed and ready to cheer for their teams. Even if your team loses, they're no more than a game out of first place. And that rookie prospect you wanted to see looks like a future star who's certain to help turn fortunes around.

Not every team plays on Opening Day. In fact those that do will have the next day off, while those that didn't, play their first game of the year, making Opening Day a magically multiple-day affair. Presto – more fans fill stands and parking lots across the country, taking their turn to celebrate the new.

That old "hope springs eternal" thing is cranked up to peak

emotional level and everyone is talking baseball.

Almost every team has a plan and some hope of making the playoffs. For those eventually falling short, "wait till next year" isn't all that bad a way to spend a summer when you can still party in the parking lot and watch the team grow together as young players develop.

Meanwhile, all around the country, the entire network that comprises our national pastime is kicking into gear. The littlest of players will soon be playing tee ball, taking swings and learning the basics of how to hit, field, throw, and record an out. For slightly older kids, coach-pitch leagues take it to the next level, in preparation for Little League and other variations of the game employing 60-foot base paths and infield diamonds with 40 feet or so from home plate to the pitching rubber.

Middle-schoolers are making decisions whether to play softball or hardball. Girls and boys everywhere are carrying on the traditions of the game. Some may choose not to play, and become fans. Others might decide the game really doesn't appeal to them. But even those who play just a bit when they're very young will walk away understanding the concept of teamwork and how to get along for the better of the group as a whole.

For those who choose to keep playing, opportunities continue through high school and college, not just for the school team, but at the intramural and even social levels. It's with these informal extensions of the game where baseball separates from other sports and embeds itself in the soil of our social landscape. Company teams, town leagues, my office against your office – it goes on and on as it has for decades and centuries.

Elements of the game were brought to what would become the Americas by colonists who discovered that even indigenous tribes had games involving the striking of spherical objects with sticks. No doubt people from across the globe were also playing games that involved the kicking of larger, inflated spheres, the first of which were believed to be pig bladders. But regardless of how other games evolved over time, no game invites us to play it in some form across the entirety of our lives in quite the same way as baseball.

I recall at a young age, 11 or so, watching my first old-timers' game at Yankee Stadium. It involved retired Yankees playing a team comprised of former opponents. It lasted maybe three innings. But the point isn't how long it lasted, but that it could be played at all, and that fans flocked to the ballpark to watch yesterday's heroes engage in an absolutely meaningless exhibition. The other compelling element was the joy with which these former professionals participated.

No other sport can attract former players to compete against each other for the sheer joy of it, a joy shared by fans and players alike. Let's go through the universal big five and attempt to envision it.

Football: Neither flag nor contact football would work for other than a small percentage of older, former players.

Hockey: Can you picture retirees skating, checking, and firing a puck at a goalie? Not really.

Soccer: Too much running, and someone would fall and break a hip.

Basketball: Too much running and jumping, and someone would fall and break a hip.

Tennis: Well, there's pickleball, an increasingly popular game, but one that every time I see played conjures up images of Lilliputians bouncing around atop a ping-pong table.

So revered are baseball's former players and old-timers that many successful older fans are willing to plunk down thousands of dollars to attend fantasy camps just to hang out with and play alongside idols of their youth. The intent is not to berate these other sports, but to point out that they have limited attraction as we get older, primarily because most don't lend themselves to modification. The only game that invites us to play it as we grow older to the extent that baseball does is golf, which requires far more land and money than any form of baseball.

Prior to packing up my glove and heading south, I stumbled across a celebrity softball game on television. It was hosted by Donald Driver, a former Green Bay Packers wide receiver and a member of the Green Bay Packers Hall of Fame. The game was a replay of an annual event to benefit Driver's Houston-based foundation. It's worth noting that these were football players coming together and having fun playing softball, not some variation of the game they played professionally. Moreover, for some of the pricier seats, fans receive autographed balls – softballs.

Baseball will always be our national game, because it was created here and continues to evolve. We exported it to other countries and it now has roots and is growing around the world in ways that are unprecedented. Is there a bigger sport in Japan? If your answer is Sumo Wrestling, my response is "good one!"

In spite of not being able to find a comfortable home on the calendar, the World Baseball Classic continues to garner growing participation and interest, while shaking its image as a glorified exhibition. A total of 84 confederation teams from five regions (Asia, the Americas, Africa, Europe, and Oceania) participate in the qualifying process for tournament group play.

Television viewing and attendance have continued to increase since the first tournament was held in 2006, as has interest among major-league caliber players, especially American players, who along with their owners, lacked enthusiasm for the event in the early going. America and the Dominican Republic have secured one title each, with Japan winning three, including the most recent.

As a result, the Classic has survived growing pains to become an anticipated event that is developing a unique history of its own, while evolving into a heated competition that involves the element of growing national pride. Even Big League team owners have begrudgingly accepted that their big-money contract players want to play in it, where in the past many had declined due to risk of injury.

In the end, all sports have value in our national and global landscapes, though in our tendency to rank things, baseball may have gotten a bad rap. It seems the rush to label games as too boring or too long and baseball as a whole no longer relevant in the way it once was were simply premature and ill advised. Rules to encourage quicker play and shorter games appear to be working. Initial reports show the average nine-inning contest is now being played in approximately 30 fewer minutes than in 2022. Not only are they being played in less time, but in-game action is on the rise and internal play is faster-paced.

That's it for closing thoughts I carry into this and future seasons as a fan. Meanwhile, I must also admit that I miss playing ball two days a week. I especially miss the sense of team. I guess I've come to realize over the course of my life that there are few places where I feel more connected to this planet, as well as other human beings, than when I'm standing on or near a baseball field.

As for Bader, life in the basement is over. I do admit, though that when the Yankees placed his namesake on waivers near the end of the 2023 season, I briefly considered a change of names to Bernie (as in Bernie Williams). But the fact remains that Harrison and I grew up in the same town, and so the impulse proved to be a passing one. Bader resides in a warm area of my home's main living space where the air doesn't attack leather so harshly. I keep my hat and jersey there too for company. I guess I've contracted a mild case of whatever Mike Gallego suffered from when he played. I also can't stop thinking of Jim Neuser and what he said about how he believes continuing to play ball has added at least 10 years to his 89-year-old life.

That's enough incentive to get me thinking that maybe this past season wasn't my last. I might not have 7 kids, 10 grandkids and 22 great grandchildren, but I do have a year-old grandson.

Maybe a little softball every year will help keep me around long enough to see him head off to college.

Hope springs eternal.

The 2023 Phillies of the Naples Super Senior Softball League. Kneeling (from left): Bob Voss, Ron Lograsso, Gary Reizen, Howard Goldstone, manager, and Jim Hunsicker. Standing, (from left) Jim Heckel, Sandy Hoad, Gary Rocco, Phil Nero, Tommy Turton, Dave Smith, Jim Neuser, Sid Steinberger, and Angelo Vitale. (missing: Noah Clark) (Photo by Bob Gentile)

Team Rosters 2023 Naples Super 60 Softball

CARDINALS: Mike Caprio (manager), David Carnall, Andre Dalpe, Richard Eudicone, Tom Fazio, Butch Fischman, Francis Gallagher, David Jeffery, Keith Klintworth, Don Leisey, Dave Martha, Jim Napier, Tony Nasralla, Ben Tantillo, Dennis Voulopos.

CUBS: Jim Pleiman (manager), Steve Doler, Dennis Fecci, William Granata, Gerry Hoogland, Don Howard, Peter Kearns, Bob Kruczowy, Paul Magrone, Dick Perkins, Tim Pratt, Bill Shields, Tony Vaccariello, Rick Watson, Ray Zajac.

DODGERS: Bob Macmillan (manager), Mike Albano, Wayne Barrick, Don Brennan, Brian Cooke, Joe Hanley, Neil Hogan, Bob Huber, Marcel Lebrun, Bob Mooney, Jerry Pyter, Craig Robinson, John Truitt, John Wolfe, David Yonvonovich.

ORIOLES: Mark Lauer (manager), Tim Bothof, John Byrum, Gary Connolly, James Dean, James Ford, Jack Galante, Bob Hollis, Ken Hughes, Gary Johnson, Ed Kinder, Kevin Loftus, Bob Pelletier, Mike Reeve, Sam Roberts, Wayne Vail.

PHILLIES: Howard Goldstone (manager), Noah Clark, Sandy Hoad, Jim Heckel, Jim Hunsicker, Ron Lograsso, Phil Nero, Jim Neuser, Gary Reizen, Gary Rocco, Dave Smith, Sid Steinberger, Tommy Turton, Angelo Vitale, Bob Voss.

RED SOX: Ray Waechter (manager) – Mark Baumgarten, Tim Cannon, Mike Conner, John Coyle, Mike Kane, Bob Kazin, John Ketterman, Greg Klein, Bill Lepore, Seager Liebig, Sharon Luebbert, John Scola. Don Seager.

ROYALS: Les Shark (manager) – Mike Crimmins, Tim Getty, Peter Kozura, Kathy Locke, John Luzi, Mark Mayer, Chuck Mayer, Dale Ribaudo, Tony Roncone, Joe Russell, Randy Segalla, Brian Starkey, Steve Vaughn.

TIGERS: Ed Voloviek (manager) – Russ Barber, Anne Brooks, Rich Cichon, Lou Federico, Ann Koenig, James Means, Dominick Mento, Russ Papa, Dave Sibits, John Simms, Eli Solomon, Ted Stewart, Bert Stohrer, Jim Volk.

YANKEES: Mark Malencia (manager) – Paul Adamowicz, Ralph Buelow, Rick Discenza, Ron Fererro, John Jackson, Nick Layton, Bob Linekin, Conrad Madaleno, Dave Marcus, Pat Moran, Dan Rowell, Cliff Small, Kim Souza.

UMPIRES
Mike Peluse, Mike Mattish, Doyle Stephens, Randy Segalla

The Kraken 2023 Roster

Joe Pignatano (manager), Nathan Cox, Martin Kurtz, Bruce Ingleright, Phil Viar, Max Troiano, John Pearson, Brandon Coraluzzo, Dany Rivera, Peter Rivera, Gabriel Castellano, Oscar Castellanos, Armando Castellanos, Christian Cotto.

A SCRAPBOOK

THE 2023 KRAKEN AND PHILLIES

Christian Cotto (left) and Oscar Castellanos.

*Martin Kurtz, president of Naples Girls Softball,
at bat with the Kraken, the amateur baseball
team he helped organize.*

*(From left) Dany Rivera, Brandon Coraluzzo, and
Peter Rivera in between innings in a Kraken game.*

Max Troiano holds court in the dugout.

Infielder Sid Steinberger on deck.

Tommy Turton practicing his throw from deep short (left). Pitcher Dave Smith (below) warming up before a game. (Photos by Bob Gentile)

ABOUT THE AUTHOR

Phil Nero is a retired journalist and writer. A transplanted New Yorker now with longstanding ties to the Midwest, he spends his days thinking about his golf swing and his nights dreaming about baseball and a more peaceful world.